The Blue and the Gray
on the
Silver Screen

The Blue and the Gray on the Silver Screen

More Than Eighty Years of Civil War Movies

Roy Kinnard

A Birch Lane Press Book
Published by Carol Publishing Group

A Birch Lane Press Book
Published by Carol Publishing Group
Birch Lane Press is a registered trademark of Carol Communications, Inc.

For editorial, sales and distribution, and queries regarding rights and permissions,
write to Carol Publishing Group, 120 Enterprise Avenue, Secaucus, N.J. 07094

In Canada: Canadian Manda Group, One Atlantic Avenue,
Suite 105, Toronto, Ontario M6K 3E7

Carol Publishing Group books are available at special discounts for bulk
purchases, sales promotion, fund-raising, or educational purposes.
Special editions can be created to specifications.

Designed by Andrew B. Gardner

Manufactured in the United States of America

10   9   8   7   6   5   4 3   2   1

Library of Congress Cataloging-in-Publication Data

Kinnard, Roy, 1952–
     The blue and the gray on the silver screen : more than eighty years of Civil War movies /
Roy Kinnard.
        P.   cm.
     "A Birch Lane Press Book."
     ISBN 1–55972–383–1 (hc)
     1. United States—History—Civil War, 1861-1865—Motion pictures and the war.
2. War films United States—History.   I. Title.
E656.K56   1996
973.7—dc20   96-31476
                                                                          CIP

For Bruce and Sara DePuye

Contents

CONTENTS

ACKNOWLEDGMENTS

*T*he author would like to thank the following individuals and organizations for their help in either acquiring photos or providing information for this book: Allied Artists, Avco-Embassy, Eddie Brandt's Saturday Matinee, Buena Vista, Cinema Collectors, Cinerama Releasing, Tony Clay, Columbia Pictures, Tony Crnkovich, Fanfare, Film Favorites, M.Sgt. Russell C. Maheras, M-G-M, National General, New Line Cinema, Jerry Ohlinger, Orion Pictures, Paramount Pictures, Republic Pictures, Stephen Sally, Maurice Terenzio, TriStar, Turner Pictures, 20th Century-Fox, United Artists, Universal Pictures, the University of Wisconsin at Madison (Iconographics Department), Jerry Vermilye, Richard Vitone, and Warner Bros. And special thanks to my editor at Citadel Press, Allan J. Wilson.

North and South: *Genie Francis, Jean Simmons, Patrick Swayze, Leslie-Anne Down*

INTRODUCTION:
THE CIVIL WAR IN THE MOVIES

"No state, upon its own mere action,
can lawfully get out of the Union."

*T*hose
words were delivered by Abraham Lincoln in his inaugural address of
March 4, 1861, when he assumed office as the sixteenth president of the
United States. Elected the previous November 6 on an antislavery
Republican ticket, Lincoln's bold opposition to the already centuries old
institution of slavery was an immediate social and political catalyst, ignit-
ing divisive, long-festering sentiments on both sides of the debate.

After perfunctory exchanges between Southern mobs and Union
troops, the Civil War officially began when South Carolina demanded the
surrender of Fort Sumter, bombing the installation on April 12, 1861.
Lincoln immediately declared a "state of insurrection" and called for sev-
enty-five thousand three-month volunteer soldiers. The United States of
America had been torn asunder, was at war with itself, and would nearly
self-destruct before Confederate general Robert E. Lee surrendered to
Union general Ulysses S. Grant on April 9, 1865.

During the Civil War the social and economic fabric of America
would be shredded not by a sinister foreign enemy invading our shores
from without but by Americans themselves from within reacting to uncon-

trollable political, financial, and racial forces. Brother would be turned against brother in a conflict so violent and so bitterly steeped in hatred that its effects still reverberated even a half century later. In some ways, they still echo today in America's continuing racial divisions and inequities.

As the Civil War itself inevitably receded into history, the stark drama inherent in the conflict was soon lifted from the cloistered domain of scholars, to be exploited by the creators of fictional drama. In the early years of the twentieth century, the newly established motion-picture industry, after first offering brief novelty shorts and crude visual records of news events and street scenes, began to experiment with narrative drama and, out of necessity, turned to theater, literature, and history for inspiration.

THE SILENT ERA

In the early years of movies, the Civil War was only forty years in the past—distant enough to be classified as "history," yet still recent enough for that bygone war to have acquired a veneer of "nostalgia," with many of the participants still living. For instance, in one early silent film, *All's Fair in Love and War* (1910), Confederate veteran John Singleton Mosby (although then past seventy) played himself. It was only natural that these pioneering filmmakers would see the Civil War as a rich source of dramatic material, with wide audience appeal, and between 1900 and 1930 literally hundreds of ten- and twenty-minute Civil War dramas as well as many features were produced by the silent-film industry. (An appendix listing Civil War films of the silent era can be found at the end of this book.)

Besides their obvious value as cinema history, many of these early films also have added unintended value as an illustration of the racial attitudes prevalent in America at the time of their production. As an example, one of the first movies dealing with issues of the Civil War era was a brief ten-minute adaptation of Harriet Beecher Stowe's 1852 novel *Uncle Tom's Cabin*, produced in 1903 by the Thomas A. Edison Co. and directed by Edwin S. Porter. This melodramatic tale of emotional turmoil among slaves of the period—and their selfless devotion to their masters—was embarrassing even in 1903, but the story's objectionable racial views didn't stop rival producer Sigmund Lubin from concocting his own version the same year under the same title, nor did it prevent subsequent remakes in 1910 (one released by Thanhouser and the other directed by J. Stuart Blackton for Vitagraph) as well as other versions in 1914 (directed by William Robert Daly for World Film Corp.), 1918 (directed by J. Searle Dawley for Famous Players-Lasky Corp.), and 1927 (directed by Harry Pollard for Universal). A latter-day reissue (with an added music and sound-effects track) of Universal's *Uncle Tom's Cabin* in the more racially aware 1950s was, to say the least, distinctly ill advised. To make matters worse, these and many other silent films, including D. W. Griffith's *Birth of a Nation* (featured later in this book) cast white actors wearing "blackface" makeup in African-American roles.

In *The Guerilla,* released by Biograph in 1908, an elderly slave actually sacrifices his own life in order to rescue his white mistress from the proverbial "fate worse than death" at the hands of a Confederate renegade. This short movie was directed by film pioneer D. W. Griffith; his innovative pictorial and editing talents would advance the visual language of screen narrative considerably over the next few years. *The Guerilla* was Griffith's first picture with a Civil War theme, and he would direct several other Civil War dramas for Biograph, including *In Old Kentucky* (1909), *The Fugitive* (1910), *The Honor of His Family* (1910), *The House With Closed Shutters* (1910), *In the Border States, or a Little Heroine of the Civil War* (1910), *The Battle* (1911), *His Trust* and a sequel, *His Trust Fulfilled* (both in 1911), *Swords and Hearts* (1911), and *The Informer* (1912) before the release of his influential (and still controversial) feature-length epic *The Birth of a Nation* in 1915.

Although Griffith's artistry is undisputed and commands respect, the dark shadow of racism taints his reputation for the modern viewer. It was in *The Birth of a Nation* that a Southern white girl commits suicide by hurling herself off a cliff rather than endure rape at the hands of a rebellious slave (played by white actor Walter Long in blackface). Griffith's racial attitudes, though, were those of a white Southerner born in the nineteenth century and, although racist to the modern viewer, were (sadly) the commonplace, *majority* point of view when *The Birth of a Nation* was made in

1915. This is said in an effort to *explain*—not *excuse*—much of white America's racial outlook at the time, and there are many such embarrassing moments in American films of the silent period and even in the sound era, with Clark Gable flippantly referring to a slave as "an ignorant darkie" in *Gone With the Wind* (1939). Also , a remarkable number of Civil War films—both silent and sound—were, if not exactly in *agreement* with the Southern "cause" during the war, then certainly in *sympathy* with the defeated Confederacy.

Although he did not equal Griffith in artistry, Thomas H. Ince was, in his time, an equally ambitious producer who was almost as noteworthy. Like Griffith, Ince realized that movies would have to be produced with larger budgets and expanded beyond their short-subject origins if they were ever to be accorded any respect by either the press or the public. In the 1912–13 period, Ince was responsible for such Civil War–oriented shorts as *The Drummer of the 8th, On Secret Service, A True Believer,* and *The Little Turncoat* before going on to direct the hour-long *Battle of Gettysburg* for Mutual in 1913. Sidney J. Olcott was another notable early filmmaker eventually overshadowed by Griffith; besides the groundbreaking religious epic *From the Manger to the Cross* (1912), Olcott also directed the one-reel Civil War drama *The Girl Spy* (Kalem, 1909), which inspired an entire series of "girl spy" Civil War shorts released by Kalem.

Other remarkable silent Civil War films made after *The Birth of a Nation* included *The Coward* (Triangle, 1915), *The Heart of Maryland* (Tiffany, 1915—later remade in 1921 and 1927), *The Warrens of Virginia* (Paramount, 1915—directed by Cecil B. DeMille and later remade in 1924), *The Crisis* (Selig, 1916), *Rose of the South* (Vitagraph, 1916), *The Field of Honor* (Universal, 1917), *Hay Foot, Straw Foot* (Paramount, 1919—a comedy starring Charles Ray), *Secret Service* (Paramount, 1919—later remade as a 1931 sound film), *The Copperhead* (Paramount, 1920—starring Lionel Barrymore), *Held by the Enemy* (Paramount, 1920), and *The Little Shepherd of Kingdom Come* (Goldwyn, 1920—later remade in 1928, and again as a sound film in 1961).

Both *The Littlest Rebel* (Photoplay Productions, 1914) and *Barbara Fritchie* (Metro, 1915) were also remade as more elaborate pictures. *The Littlest Rebel* was reworked as a Shirley Temple sound film by 20th

Scarlett: *Timothy Dalton*

Century–Fox in 1935, and the 1915 *Barbara Fritchie*, which had starred Mary Miles Minter as the title heroine in a tale of star-crossed lovers separated by the Civil War, was remade by Producers Distributing Corporation in 1924, with Florence Vidor starring in the new version.

The late silent era also saw the release of three other Civil War movies deserving mention. The best of these, Buster Keaton's feature-length comedy *The General* (United Artists, 1927)—discussed later in this book—was an intelligent and slickly produced farce, offering an accurate and highly detailed vision of the war in the bargain.

Abraham Lincoln (Associated First National Pictures, 1924) was an ambitious, episodic biography outlining the sixteenth president's life from boyhood to his assassination. George A. Billings (who specialized in the role) starred as Lincoln, with Phil Rosen directing from a script by Frances Marion. Although slowly and deliberately paced, the film was lavishly mounted by producers Al and Ray Rockett, garnering much-deserved praise for the historical accuracy of its costumes and sets.

Hands Up! (Paramount, 1926) was a sophisticated comedy starring Raymond Griffith. Although forgotten today, Raymond Griffith was popular in silents and later became a successful producer in the sound era. In *Hands Up!* President Lincoln (again played by George A. Billings) dispatches Griffith to the West in order to secure a gold mine intended to finance the Union war effort, with a Rebel spy in close pursuit. *Hands Up!* was directed by Clarence Badger, from a screenplay by Monty Brice and Lloyd Corrigan, adapted from a story by Reginald Morris.

THE SOUND ERA

With the coming of the sound era in Hollywood and the restrictive financial difficulties brought about by the Great Depression, movie producers tended to downplay the epic film, aside from those "epics" that could achieve the *illusion* of grandeur and scope without ever leaving the back lot, through the economical use of miniatures, optical effects, and stock footage. A typical example would be Cecil B. DeMille's 1934 production of *Cleopatra*, which, although filmed on a larger-than-average budget for that time, was still cost-conscious in its use of stock footage from DeMille's 1923 silent version of *The Ten Commandments* in order to expand the battle scenes.

The Civil War pictures made in the 1930s were generally small-scale in concept, designed to function as either romances (like *Carolina* and *So Red the Rose*) or spy dramas *(Secret Service* and *Operator 13),* avoiding lengthy (and costly) battle scenes wherever possible. Aside from the 1930 rerelease (with an added music and sound-effects track) of D. W. Griffith's *Birth of a Nation,* the only Civil War–oriented film showing any real epic sweep was Griffith's underrated biopic *Abraham Lincoln* (1930), that is, until the release of producer David O. Selznick's *Gone With the Wind* at the very end of the decade. Even though the early sound Civil War films may have fallen short in terms of physical *scale,* however, the *emotional* impact of the Civil War was illustrated by movies like *So Red the Rose,* and since the lasting impact of *any* war is felt—and remembered—in personal human terms, this approach was, in its own way, very effective.

Other 1930s Civil War films of note included the Marion Davies–Gary Cooper showcase *Operator 13* (M-G-M, 1934); *The Littlest Rebel* (20th Century–Fox, 1935), starring Shirley Temple; *The Prisoner of Shark Island* (20th Century–Fox, 1936), directed by John Ford; and a fine study of Abraham Lincoln's early years, *Young Mr. Lincoln* (20th Century–Fox, 1939), starring Henry Fonda and also directed by John Ford.

Almost as if to compensate for any previous lack of budgetary opulence, Hollywood's most famous dramatization of the Civil War—*Gone With the Wind* (1939)—brought the full tragedy of the War Between the States to vibrant life for a new generation, depicting the enormous physical dimensions of that conflict in lush Technicolor brilliance—while still offering an abundance of emotional fireworks in the process. In many ways, Selznick's epic is still the best film ever made on the subject. *Gone With the Wind* was so impressive, so successful, and so widely *seen* that it was virtually the last word in Civil War movies. In the 1940s and 1950s, Hollywood Civil War films tended to be, again, small-scale human dramas, with an occasional big-budget attempt to emulate Selznick's masterpiece. A spate of lavish westerns had been initiated with the Technicolor Errol Flynn vehicle *Dodge City* (Warner Bros., 1939), and *Dark Command* (Republic, 1940), *Santa Fe Trail* (Warner Bros., 1940), and *Virginia City* (Warner Bros., 1940) were all expensively produced Civil War movies fol-

lowing this trend. Both *Tap Roots* (Universal, 1948) and the later Elizabeth Taylor vehicle *Raintree County* (M-G-M, 1957) were extravagant Technicolor productions that tried to duplicate the *Gone With the Wind* formula, with only partial success.

Director John Huston's superlative *Red Badge of Courage* (M-G-M, 1951), while staging some excellent battle scenes inspired by Matthew Brady's Civil War–era photographs, examined the war in microcosm through the emotional toll it exacted on the individual soldiers involved. Although M-G-M reedited and shortened the picture from Huston's original cut before release, *The Red Badge of Courage* is a fine character study, remaining one of the best Civil War (and *antiwar*) films made in Hollywood.

Other memorable Civil War films of the 1940s and 1950s included the Red Skelton comedy *A Southern Yankee* (M-G-M, 1948), the Gary Cooper vehicles *Springfield Rifle* (Warner Bros., 1952) and *Friendly Persuasion* (Allied Artists, 1956), and *Band of Angels* (Warner Bros., 1957), starring Clark Gable in a role influenced by his Rhett Butler characterization in *Gone With the Wind* and one of the first Civil War movies to contain progressive racial attitudes.

THE "MODERN" CIVIL WAR FILM

With the collapse of Hollywood's studio system in the late 1950s and early 1960s and the rise of independent film production, movies gradually became more "realistic" in tone, more willing to examine difficult political and social issues than films of previous decades, and by nature more cynical and even pessimistic. Significantly, most older Civil War films—until recent productions like *Glory* (Tri-Star, 1989)—had not really dealt with the basic social, racial, and political causes of the war but had, for the most part, used the war as a period backdrop for costume drama or romance, providing entertainment while offering minimal insight into a fascinating and tumultuous period of American history. Such 1960s and 1970s films as *Major Dundee* (Columbia, 1965), *Shenandoah* (Universal, 1965), *Alvarez Kelly* (Columbia, 1966), *The Good, the Bad, and the Ugly* (United Artists, 1967), and *The Beguiled* (Universal 1971) took a much darker, almost revisionist look

at the Civil War than had their cinematic forebears.

Hollywood's fascination with the Civil War continues today, with TV miniseries like *The Blue and the Gray* (1982) with Stacy Keach; *North and South* (1985) and *North and South, Book II* (1986), both with Patrick Swayze; made-for-TV movies like *The Rose and the Jackal* (1990), with Christopher Reeve; the recent *Andersonville* (1996); as well as theatrical features like *Gettysburg* (1993) and documentarian Ken Burns's excellent TV history of the war creating further interest. Even Selznick's monolithic *Gone With the Wind,* kept before the public eye with constant reissues and TV showings, was "updated" and "expanded" with the production of a controversial TV miniseries sequel, *Scarlett* (1994), starring Joanne Whalley-Kilmer as Scarlett O'Hara and Timothy Dalton as Rhett Butler.

But whatever the reason for the current interest in the Civil War as "entertainment," whether spurred by a simple, unadorned fascination with history or by parallels with our own recent Vietnam era, that interest continues and is reflected in Hollywood's ongoing exploitation of the subject.

What follows is a pictorial history of theatrical feature films dealing with the Civil War or Civil War–era figures, selected either for their direct relation to the history of the war or for their representation of the personalities that dominated that turbulent era.

The Films

The Birth of a Nation: *Mae Marsh*

THE BIRTH OF A NATION

1915 • Epoch Producing Corp.

CREDITS

Presented by: David Wark Griffith; producer: David Wark Griffith; director: David Wark Griffith; assistant directors: Thomas E. O'Brien and George Andre Beranger; screenplay: David Wark Griffith and Frank E. Woods (based on the novels *The Clansman* and *The Leopard's Spots,* both by Thomas Dixon); photography: G. W. Bitzer; assistant cameraman: Karl Brown; costumes: Goldstein Co., Los Angeles; musical accompaniment: Joseph Carl Breil.
Length: 12 reels.
Released February 8, 1915.

CAST

Henry B. Walthall *(Col. Ben Cameron)*, Miriam Cooper *(Margaret Cameron)*, Mae Marsh *(Flora Cameron)*, Josephine Crowell *(Mrs. Cameron)*, Spottiswoode Aitken *(Dr. Cameron)*, J. A. Beringer *(Wade Cameron)*, Maxfield Stanley *(Duke Cameron)*, Jennie Lee *(Mammy)*, Ralph Lewis *(Hon. Austin Stoneman)*, Lilian Gish *(Elsie Stoneman)*, Elmer Clifton *(Phil Stoneman)*, Robert Harron *(Tod Stoneman)*, Wallace Reid *(Jeff)*, Mary Alden *(Lydia Brown)*, George Siegmann *(Silas Lynch)*, Walter Long *(Gus)*, Joseph Henabery *(Abraham Lincoln)*, Raoul Walsh *(John Wilkes Booth)*, Donald Crisp *(Gen. Ulysses S. Grant)*, Howard Gaye *(Gen. Robert E. Lee)*, Sam de Grasse *(Charles Sumner)*, William DeVaull *(Nelse)*, William Freeman *(Jake)*, Thomas Wilson *(Stoneman's Servant)*, with Fred Burns, Allan Sears, and Elmo Lincoln.

*T*he

Birth of a Nation, director D. W. Griffith's epic, was released in 1915 and was an immediate sensation with both the press and the public, due, it should be noted, more to its strong artistic qualities than its controversial racial attitudes. Griffith's Civil War drama lends a human dimension to the conflict by representing events through the eyes of two families, the Stonemans and the Camerons, as the Confederacy is defeated, invaded by carpetbaggers, and finally overrun and exploited by liberated slaves— until order is restored by the Ku Klux Klan. The film was based on Thomas Dixon's novel *The Clansman*, published in 1905, and also derived material from Dixon's earlier, and undeniably racist, novel *The Leopard's Spots*, published in 1902.

It was Griffith's cinematic artistry that ensured the film's success, but it was his heroic treatment of the Ku Klux Klan that made *The Birth of a Nation* so controversial in its day—even provoking riots in some cities— and it is this troublesome aspect of the film that prevents its widespread exhibition even today.

The Birth of a Nation, though, is over eighty years old, a basic fact that should be kept in mind when discussing the film's dated and (from a modern, enlightened perspective) offensive racial attitudes. Regrettably, when the film was made, Griffith's racial views reflected those of the majority.

What remains fresh and vibrant about the movie even now, however, is Griffith's impressive filmmaking craftsmanship and editorial technique, his flawless, painterly visual compositions, and his forceful narrative. The acting is (at various times) both overwrought and surprisingly naturalistic and understated, and the primary cast—Henry B. Walthall, Miriam Cooper, Mae Marsh, and Lillian Gish—already Griffith veterans from his short subjects, became household names due to the film's widespread success.

With *The Birth of a Nation*, D. W. Griffith took the motion-picture industry, as well as his own career, out of the doldrums of the nickelodeon era, propelling movies onward and upward to the status of a new art

The Birth of a Nation: *Walter Long* (center), *apprehended by the Klan*

form. Upon viewing this film at the White House on February 18, 1915, President Woodrow Wilson was said to have commented: "It is like writing history with lightning, and my only regret is that it is all so terribly true." Although later proved apocryphal, these words reflect the impact *The Birth of a Nation* had at that time.

Reviews

"The Birth of a Nation, *an elaborate new motion picture taken on an ambitious scale . . . is a film version of some of the melodramatic and inflammatory material contained in* The Clansman, *by Thomas Dixon. A great deal might be said concerning the spirit revealed in Mr. Dixon's review of the unhappy chapter of Reconstruction and concerning the sorry service rendered by its plucking at old wounds. But of the film as a film, it*

The Birth of a Nation

may be reported simply that it is an impressive new illustration of the scope of the motion picture camera."
—*NEW YORK TIMES, MARCH 4, 1915*

"The Birth of a Nation . . . *received its first New York public presentation in the Liberty Theatre, New York, March 3. The daily newspaper reviewers pronounced it as the last word in picture making."*
—*VARIETY, MARCH 12, 1915*

"The war scenes present the Griffith technique on a broader scale than it has ever been seen."
—*NEW YORK DRAMATIC MIRROR, MARCH 10, 1915*

THE GENERAL

1927 • United Artists

CREDITS

Producer: Joseph M. Schenk; director: Buster Keaton; screenplay:
Buster Keaton and Clyde Bruckman (adaptation by Al Boasberg and
Charles Smith); photography: J. Devereaux Jennings and
Bert Haines; lighting effects: Denver Harmon;
technical director: Fred Gabourie; film editor: Sherman Kell;
assistant editor: Harry Barnes; makeup: Fred C. Ryle.
Length: 8 reels (7,500 feet). Released February 5, 1927.

CAST

Buster Keaton *(Johnny Gray)*, Glen Cavender *(Captain Anderson)*, Jim
Farley *(General Thatcher)*, Frederick Vroom *(Southern General)*, Marion
Mack *(Annabelle Lee)*, Charles Smith *(Her Father)*, Frank Barnes *(Her
Brother)*, with Joseph Keaton, Mike Donlin, and Tom Nawn
(Union Generals).

*I*n

The General, comedian Buster Keaton starred as young railroad engineer Johnnie Gray, who wants to enlist in the Confederate army when he winds up in Georgia at the outbreak of the Civil War but is deferred because his profession is vital to the war effort. When Johnnie's girlfriend, Annabelle (Marion Mack), travels to Georgia in order to visit her father, Union soldiers hijack the train she is on, and Johnnie pursues them in another locomotive (the film's title refers to a train), crossing over into Union territory during the chase. Johnnie rescues Annabelle and returns with her aboard the locomotive, followed by Union troops. Disclosing Union plans to a Confederate officer, who then wins a battle as a result, Johnnie is awarded a commission as a lieutenant and gains Annabelle's devotion.

Directed by Keaton, *The General* was not only a great comedy but one of the best films of any type made during the silent era, with a tight, believable plot that can stand on its own in a dramatic sense and an admirable historical verisimilitude. Keaton was a master craftsman, and the intricate sight gags in this and many of his other films have a balletic grace and precision unmatched by his rival comics.

Nevertheless, Keaton's career declined in the sound era, largely due to his alcoholism and lack of business acumen. By the late 1930s he was appearing in comedy shorts for Columbia, one of which, *Moochin' Through Georgia* (1939), had a Civil War theme and dimly recalled his glory days in *The General*.

The basic story line of *The General*, derived from an actual historical event of the Civil War, had been used once before in *Railroad Raiders of '62* (Kalem, 1911) and would be again, in 1956, in the live-action Walt Disney feature *The Great Locomotive Chase*.

Although Keaton is universally hailed today as a creative genius, his films were not always well received by the critics when originally released, as is indicated by the mixed reviews below.

The General: *Buster Keaton*

Reviews

"There are some corking gags in the picture, but as they are all a part of the chase, they are over-shadowed. There isn't a single bit in the picture that brings a real howl. . . . No one besides the star has a chance to do anything. . . . Marion Mack looks as if she might register if given a chance."
—VARIETY, FEBRUARY 9, 1927

"In spite of his bursts of speed and flashes of ingenuity, Johnnie Gray, the hero of The General *. . . is hardly the person who would be trusted with a*

Moochin' Through Georgia: *One of Keaton's later, inferior comedy shorts*

locomotive. This role is played by Buster Keaton, who appears to have bit-
ten off more than he can chew in this farcical affair concerned with the days
of the Civil War. Mr. Keaton still preserves his inscrutable expression;
he looks like a clergyman and acts like a vaudeville tumbler.
. . . The production itself is singularly well-mounted. . . .
—NEW YORK TIMES, FEBRUARY 8, 1927

"They're kidding everything now and any day you may expect to see U. S.
Grant and Robert E. Lee break into a Charleston. Not that they do it in
The General, *but Buster Keaton does spoof the Civil War most uncivilly*
in his new comedy."
—PHOTOPLAY, MARCH 1927

The General: *Buster Keaton*

"One of Keaton's best silent features. . . . Not as fanciful as other Keaton films, but beautifully done."
—LEONARD MALTIN, LEONARD MALTIN'S TV MOVIES AND VIDEO GUIDE

Abraham Lincoln: *Ian Keith, Kay Hammond, and Walter Huston*

ABRAHAM LINCOLN

1930 • United Artists

CREDITS

Director: D. W. Griffith; screenplay: Stephen Vincent Benet;
photography: Karl Struss; film editor: John Considine Jr.;
music: Hugo Reisenfeld; set designer: William Cameron Menzies.
Running time: 97 minutes.

CAST

Walter Huston *(Abraham Lincoln)*, Una Merkel *(Ann Rutledge)*, Kay
Hammond *(Mary Todd Lincoln)*, E. Alyn Warren *(Stephen Douglas)*,
Hobart Bosworth *(Gen. Robert E. Lee)*, Fred Warren *(Gen. Ulysses S.
Grant)*, Henry B. Walthall *(Colonel Marshall)*, Frank Campeau *(General
Sheridan)*, Francis Ford *(Sheridan's Aide)*, W. L. Thorne *(Tom Lincoln)*,
Ian Keith *(John Wilkes Booth)*, Oscar Apfel *(Stanton)*, Otto Hoffman
(Offut), Edgar Deering *(Armstrong)*, Russell Simpson *(Lincoln's
Employer)*, Helen Ware *(Mrs. Edwards)*, Charles Crockett *(Sheriff)*,
Jason Robards Sr. *(Herndon)*, Gordon Thorpe *(Tad Lincoln)*, James
Bradbury Sr. *(General Scott)*, Cameron Prudhomme *(John Hay)*,
Jimmy Eagles *(Young Soldier)*, with Hank Bell, Carl Stockdale,
George McQuarrie, Ralph Lewis, and Robert Brower.

*I*n *Abraham Lincoln,* director D. W. Griffith certainly proved his mastery over the new sound medium. Individual scenes, such as Sheridan's ride through the Shenandoah Valley and the Civil War battle sequences, are fluid and powerful; in fact, the direction is much more effective than that of many other early talkies. The problem with *Abraham Lincoln* is that Griffith was forced into an episodic treatment of Lincoln's life by the executives in charge at United Artists, resulting in a loose, disconnected narrative.

Walter Huston was well cast as Lincoln, but his performance is reduced to stiff posturing in the later scenes depicting Lincoln as president, as though Griffith were in such awe of his subject that he was afraid to breathe life into him and simply allow Huston to interpret Lincoln as a human being. Kay Hammond was ideally cast as Mary Todd Lincoln, but in the scenes depicting Lincoln as a young man, Una Merkel was far less suited to the role of Ann Rutledge, doomed to an early death.

Karl Struss's excellent photography is one of the film's strong points, a facet often lost in the flat-contrast public-domain prints generally available today. *Abraham Lincoln* is a structurally flawed picture, but this shortcoming was hardly attributable to Griffith , who did not enjoy total artistic control; nevertheless, the film is still a remarkable achievement and is definitely worth a viewing.

Reviews

"David Wark Griffith, the old master of the early silent screen, presented . . . an episodical conception of the life of Abraham Lincoln. It is quite a worthy pictorial offering with a genuinely fine and inspiring performance by Walter Huston. . . ."
—NEW YORK TIMES, AUGUST 26, 1930

"More than an outstanding classic of sound pictures, Abraham Lincoln *eclipses the most conservative illusion of a modernized* Birth of a Nation. *It is a startlingly superlative accomplishment. . . ."*
—VARIETY, AUGUST 27, 1930

Abraham Lincoln: *Walter Huston and Una Merkel*

Only the Brave: *Mary Brian and Gary Cooper*

ONLY THE BRAVE

1930 • Paramount

CREDITS

Director: Frank Tuttle; screenplay: Edward E. Paramore Jr., Agnes
Brand Leahy, and Richard H. Digges Jr. (based on a story by
Keene Thompson); photography: Harry Fischbeck;
film editor: Doris Drought.
Running time: 66 minutes.

CAST

Gary Cooper *(Capt. James Braydon)*, Mary Brian *(Barbara Calhoun)*,
Phillips Holmes *(Capt. Robert Darrington)*, James Neill
(Vance Calhoun), Morgan Farley *(Tom Wendell)*, Guy Oliver
(Gen. Ulysses S. Grant), John H. Elliott *(Gen. Robert E. Lee)*,
E. H. Calvert *(The Colonel)*, Virginia Bruce *(Elizabeth)*, Elda Voelkel
(Lucy Cameron), William Le Maire *(The Sentry)*, Freeman S. Wood
(Elizabeth's Lover), Lalo Encinas *(General Grant's Secretary)*,
Clinton Rosemond *(Butler)*,
William Bakewell *(Young Lieutenant)*.

"Stand back—or I'll shoot—"

Only the Brave: *Gary Cooper, Phillips Holmes, and Mary Brian*

A_n

uninspired spy drama with a Civil War background, *Only the Brave* presents Gary Cooper in the role of a Union agent who, operating incognito behind enemy lines, falls in love with Southern belle Mary Brian. Cooper is generally remembered today for his latter-day, rugged *High Noon* persona, and his early career as a fresh-faced romantic leading man has been more or less forgotten, since his late silent and early sound films are rarely screened. Cooper's star quality is fully in evidence here, but he is thwarted by a hackneyed script and Frank Tuttle's uninspired direction. The Civil War spy-romance plot had been used often in the silent era and was old hat even by 1930; both Cooper and his lovely leading lady, Mary Brian, deserved better.

Reviews

"The story is concerned with a Federal soldier who finds his sweetheart in the arms of another man. He volunteers for dangerous spy duty, which requires that he penetrate the Confederate lines and be caught, so that the plans he carries sewed in the lining of his coat will be discovered and mislead the enemy. . . . Mary Brian as the Southern belle is rather sugary. Gary Cooper's performance as the spy is not up to his usual standards."
—NEW YORK TIMES, MARCH 8, 1930

"Historic peace-making of Grant and Lee at Appomatox is the semi-final shot that guarantees everything. . . . Phillips Holmes and William Le Maire
rate highest among performances rendered under Cooper's and Miss Brian's."
—VARIETY, MARCH 12, 1930

Only the Brave: *Guy Oliver and Gary Cooper*

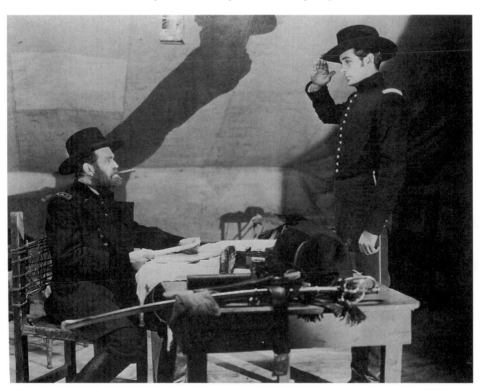

SECRET SERVICE

1931 • RKO

CREDITS

Producer: Louis Sarecky; director: J. Walter Ruben;
screenplay: Gerrit J. Lloyd and Bernard Schubert
(based on a play by William Gilette);
photography: Edward Cronjager;
film editor: John Kitchin;
art director: Max Ree.
Running time: 69 minutes.

CAST

Richard Dix *(Lewis Dumont)*, Shirley Grey *(Edith Varney)*,
William Post Jr. *(Lieutenant Dumont)*, Gavin Gordon *(Archford)*,
Fred Warren *(Gen. Ulysses S. Grant)*, Nance O'Neill *(Mrs. Varney)*,
Virginia Sale *(Miss Kittridge)*, Florence Lake *(Caroline)*,
Clarence Muse *(Jonas)*, Harold Kinney *(Howard Varney)*,
Eugene Jackson *(Israel)*, Frederick Burton *(General Randolph)*,
Carl Gerard *(Lieutenant Foray)*,
Gertrude Howard *(Martha)*,
with Emma Reed.

Secret Service: *Shirley Grey and Richard Dix*

V irtually
identical in plot to Paramount's Gary Cooper vehicle *Only the Brave,*
released the previous year, *Secret Service* is a Civil War spy drama with
iron-jawed leading man Richard Dix in the starring role. Dix plays a
Union officer sent on a espionage mission behind enemy lines along with
his brother, played by William Post Jr.; the inevitable romantic complica-
tions arise when Dix falls in love with the daughter of a Confederate general. *Secret Service* did not improve the shaky fortunes of the newly found-
ed studio RKO. The film was a remake of a 1919 silent, and the weak story
material had certainly not improved over the intervening decade. Both
film versions were based on an 1895 play by William Gillette, a revival of
which was staged by New York's Phoenix Repertory Company and
broadcast on television's *Theater in America* series on January 12, 1977.
John Lithgow and Meryl Streep starred, and between acts cast members
performed Civil War–era songs.

Reviews

"Some are likely to complain that the film has too much love and
not enough secret service."
—*NEW YORK TIMES,* DECEMBER 14, 1931

"Richard Dix does a good character in Secret Service. *It's all the*
picture has. . . . Otherwise anemic throughout, it's this star's strong
characterization that holds the interest from the outset."
—*VARIETY,* DECEMBER 15, 1931

Secret Service: *Gavin Gordon, Shirley Grey, and Richard Dix*

CAROLINA

1934 • Fox

CREDITS

Director: Henry King; screenplay: Reginald Berkeley
(based on the play *The House of Connelly* by Paul Green);
photography: Hal Mohr; film editor: Robert Bassler.
Running time: 83 minutes.

CAST

Janet Gaynor *(Joanna)*, Lionel Barrymore *(Bob Connelly)*,
Robert Young *(Will Connelly)*, Richard Cromwell *(Allen)*,
Henrietta Crosman *(Mrs. Connelly)*, Mona Barrie *(Virginia)*,
Stepin Fetchit *(Scipio)*, Russell Simpson *(Richards)*, Ronnie Cosbey
(Harry), Jackie Cosbey *(Jackie)*, Almeda Fowler *(Geraldine)*,
Alden Chase *(Jack Hampton)*, Roy Watson *(Jefferson Davis)*,
John Elliott *(Gen. Robert E. Lee)*, John Webb Dillon *(Gen. "Stonewall"
Jackson)*, J. C. Fowler *(Gen. Leonidas Polk)*, André Cheron
(General Beauregard), James Ellison *(Dancer)*, Clinton Rosemund
(Black Singer), and Shirley Temple *(Little Girl)*.

(Opposite) Carolina: *Lionel Barrymore and Janet Gaynor*

*C*arolina starred Janet Gaynor as the daughter of a farmer whose land in Pennsylvania is owned by a wealthy Southern family headed by Civil War vet Lionel Barrymore. The alcoholic Barrymore character stubbornly clings to the past, and after her father's death, Gaynor's efforts to resolve the financial problems concerning her father's property are frustrated until she falls in love with Barrymore's son, played by Robert Young, the heir to the family fortune.

A symbolic view of the fading Civil War South of a previous generation and the "marriage" of the North and South as represented by a new generation (Gaynor and Young), *Carolina* was based on the play *The House of Connelly* by Paul Green. It was this title that was used for the film's British release.

The House of Connelly was the first play produced by New York's Group Theatre. Henry King, director of *Carolina*, recalled in an interview that the Hays Office censors would not permit Fox to use the play's title for the film because a subplot in the original play dealt with miscegenation.

For the film, King and other crew members traveled to South Carolina, where background footage was shot on location and architecture was photographed for research in set design.

Reviews

"Among the leading players in Carolina, *a pictorial transcription of Paul Green's play* The House of Connelly, *is the titian-haired Janet Gaynor, who is just as fortunate in her role as she was . . . in* State Fair. *The current offering is a restrained and sensible adaptation of the story of the impoverished members of a proud old Southern family."*
—*NEW YORK TIMES*, FEBRUARY 16, 1934

Carolina: *Robert Young and Janet Gaynor*

"The first half of Carolina *is much stronger than the rest. As the
final reel is arrived at, the picture begins to lessen in impact. . . .
Barrymore plays a vet of the Civil War who has fallen to love
of liquor and, under doubtful mental balance, to disturbing
memories of the love of younger days in which
his sister interfered."*
—VARIETY, FEBRUARY 20, 1934

OPERATOR 13

1934 • M-G-M

CREDITS

Producer: Lucien Hubbard; director: Richard Boleslavsky;
screenplay: Harry Thew, Zelda Sears, and Eve Greene (based on the
novel by Robert W. Chambers); photography: George Folsey;
film editor: Frank Sullivan; art directors: Cedric Gibbons and Arnold
Gillespie; costumes: Adrian; music: Dr. William Axt;
music and lyrics: "Sleepy Head" (sung by the Mills Brothers),
"Jungle Fever," and "Once in a Lifetime" by Walter Donaldson
andGus Kahn.
Running time: 86 minutes.

CAST

Marion Davies *(Gail Loveless/"Ann Claibourne")*, Gary Cooper, *(Capt.
Jack Gailliard)*, Jean Parker, *(Eleanor)*, Katharine Alexander *(Pauline
Cushman)*, Ted Healy *(Dr. Hitchock)*, Russell Hardie *(Littledale)*, Henry
Wadsworth *(John Pelham)*, Douglas Dumbrille *(Gen. "Jeb" Stuart)*,
Willard Robertson *(Captain Channing)*, Fuzzy Knight *(Sweeney)*,
Sidney Toler *(Major Allen)*, Robert McWade *(Colonel Sharpe)*, Marjorie
Gateson *(Mrs. Shackleford)*, Wade Boteler *(Gaston)*, Walter Long
(Operator 55), Hattie McDaniel *(Cook)*, Francis McDonald, *(Denton)*,
William H. Griffith *(Mac)*, James Marcus *(Staff Colonel)*, Sam
McDaniel *(Old Bob)*, Buddy Roosevelt *(Civilian)*, Frank McGlynn Jr.
and Wheeler Oakman *(Scouts)*, Don Douglas *(Confederate Officer)*, Si
Jenks *(White Trash)*, Reginald Barlow *(Colonel Storm)*, Ernie
Alexander and Richard Powell *(Confederate Sentries)*, Belle Daube
(Mrs. Dandrige), Wilfred Lucas *(Judge)*, Bob Stevenson *(Guard)*,

Operator 13: *Marion Davies and Gary Cooper*

Operator 13: *Walter Long and Marion Davies*

Martin Turner *(Wickman)*, Frank Burt *(Confederate Lieutenant)*, Wallie
Howe *(Clergyman)*, William Henry *(Young Lieutenant)*, Richard
Tucker *(Execution Officer)*, Arthur Grant *(Chaplain)*, Sherry Tansey
(Officer), Lia Lance *(Witch Woman)*, Charles Lloyd *(Union Private)*, De
Witt C. Jennings *(Artillery Man)*, Sam Ash *(Lieutenant)*, Ernie Adams
(Orderly), Clarence Hummel Wilson *(Claybourne)*, Franklin Parker
(John Hay), Claudia Coleman *(Nurse)*, Sterling Holloway *(Wounded
Soldier)*, Sherry Hall *(Army Officer)*, Douglas Fowley *(Union Officer)*,
Fred Warren *(Gen. Ulysses S. Grant)*, John Elliott *(Gen. Robert E. Lee)*,
Frank Leighton *(Union Major)*, James C. Morton *(Secret Service Man)*,
Hattie Hill, John Kirkley *(Slaves)*, John Larkin, Poppy Wilde *(Party
Guests)*, with the Mills Brothers.

*P*aramount

loaned Gary Cooper to M-G-M for *Operator 13*, which was strictly a vehicle for Marion Davies. Davies—the real-life mistress of publishing baron
William Randolph Hearst—played a Civil War–era actress who becomes a
Union spy in yet another behind-the-lines drama. Cooper played second
fiddle to Davies here; she was, as in all her films, spotlighted by the studio

in deference to her benefactor Hearst, who wielded enormous influence in Hollywood. Davies was, in fact, very talented and adept at both comedy and drama; Hearst's tyrannical control of her career was really unnecessary, and his meddling actually did her more harm than good when she was frequently cast in inappropriate roles, selected by Hearst because the material was "respectable."

Operator 13 is a solid but unremarkable production, benefiting from the expected M-G-M gloss; George Folsey's excellent photography was nominated for an Academy Award.

One extended sequence in *Operator 13* that has undoubtedly kept the picture from receiving wide play in recent years has spy Davies going undercover while disguised in blackface!

Reviews

"In Operator 13, *a conception of the late Robert W. Chambers's romantic espionage stories of the Civil War, Marion Davies, as the central figure, appears in some scenes disguised as a mulatto. She is presumed thus to hoodwink several Southerners, including army officers, and to carry out her mission of spying with great success. Later, with fair face and golden tresses, she reappears before some of the same individuals, this time impersonating a Southern girl. . . . Although Richard Boleslavsky's direction is imaginative, there are moments when abrupt changes of scene cause the story to be somewhat confusing."*
—*NEW YORK TIMES, JUNE 23, 1934*

"One of Davies's best. Holds a lot for popular appeal and will do much to reestablish the star. Despite that it's one of those North and South Civil War romances, it's so well-done that it grips throughout. . . ."
VARIETY, JUNE 26, 1934

"Patently absurd but still somehow entertaining; fast moving and handsomely shot."
—LEONARD MALTIN, *LEONARD MALTIN'S TV MOVIES AND VIDEO GUIDE*

The Little Colonel: *Bill "Bojangles" Robinson and Shirley Temple*

THE LITTLE COLONEL

1935 • Fox

CREDITS

Director: David Butler; screenplay: William Coonselman (based on the
novel *The Little Colonel* by Annie Fellows Johnston); photography: Arthur
Miller; Technicolor sequence photography: William Skall; Technicolor
director: Natalie Kalmus; art director: William Darling; costumes: William
Lambert; musical direction: Arthur Lange; music adaptation: Cyril J.
Mockridge; sound: S. C. Chapman; assistant director: Ad Schaumer; sons:
"The Old Woman (Love's Young Dream)," Irish folk song; "God's Gwinter
Trouble de Water," Negro spiritual; "Moaning," music by Louis de
Francesco; "Sun Shines Brighter," words by William Kernell, music by
Louis de Francesco; "Little Colonel Improvisation,"
words and music by Cyril J. Mockridge.
Running time: 80 minutes.

CAST

Shirley Temple *(Lloyd Sherman)*, Lionel Barrymore *(Colonel Lloyd)*, Evelyn
Venable *(Elizabeth)*, John Lodge *(Jack Sherman)*, Sidney Blackmer *(Swayzey)*,
Alden Chase *(Hull)*, William Burress *(Dr. Scott)*, Frank Darien *(Nebler)*,
Robert Warick *(Colonel Gray)*, Hattie McDaniel *(Mom Beck)*, Geneva
Williams *(Maria)*, Avonne Jackson *(May Lily)*, Nyanza Potts *(Henry Clay)*,
Bill Robinson *(Walker)*, David O'Brien *(Frank Randolph)*, Capt. C. E.
Anderson *(Overseer)*, Lillian West *(Neighbor Woman)*, Lucille Ward *(Aunt
Sally)*, Frank Hammond *(Carriage Driver)*, Ford West *(Village Hanger-on)*,
Vester Pegg and Marty Faust *(Frontiersmen)*, John Ince *(Sheriff)*, Arthur
Stuart Hull *(Passerby)*, Frank O'Connor *(Aide)*, Richard Hamblin *(Card
Manipulator)*, Charles C. Wilson *(Higgins)*, Harry Strand *(Sergeant)*.

*T*he *Little Colonel,* an excellent Shirley Temple vehicle set during the Reconstruction period after the Civil War, is interesting in comparison with the similar Temple film *The Littlest Rebel,* also released by the same studio (after its merger with 20th Century) later that year. *The Littlest Rebel,* however, actually took place during the Civil War and deals more immediately with that conflict.

In *The Little Colonel,* Shirley's mother (Evelyn Venable), after marrying a Northerner (John Lodge), is rejected by her father (crusty Southern gentleman Lionel Barrymore), with Shirley eventually reconciling her mother and grandfather before the climactic fade-out.

Director Irving Cummings was originally slated to direct *The Little Colonel* but was replaced by David Butler before the start of filming. The last scene of *The Little Colonel* was photographed in Technicolor, and the entire film—like *The Littlest Rebel* and other Shirley Temple movies—was later colorized for video release.

Reviews

"Even nonfans should like this . . . as (Shirley) mends broken ties between Grandpa Barrymore and Mama Venable in the Reconstruction South . . . and does that famous step dance with [Bill "Bojangles"] Robinson."
—LEONARD MALTIN, *LEONARD MALTIN'S TV MOVIES AND VIDEO GUIDE*

"Fox continues to reveal ingenuity and showmanship in fitting Shirley Temple with vehicles that rate high as entertainment and preserve as well as increase the popularity of this youngster."
—*VARIETY,* MARCH 27, 1935

The Little Colonel: *Lionel Barrymore and Shirley Temple*

"All adrip with magnolia whimsy and vast, unashamed portions of synthetic Dixie atmosphere, [The Little Colonel] *allows Miss Temple to patter merrily through her distinguished repertoire."*
—NEW YORK TIMES, MARCH 22, 1935

THE LITTLEST REBEL

1935 • 20th Century–Fox

CREDITS

Producers: Darryl F. Zanuck and B. G. DeSylva; director: David Butler; screenplay: Edwin Burke and Harry Tugend (based on the play by Edward Peple); photography: John Seitz; film editor: Irene Morra; musical director; Cyril Mockridge; art director: William Darling; set designer: Thomas K. Little; costumes: Gwen Wakeling. Running time: 73 minutes.

CAST

Shirley Temple *(Virginia Huston Cary)*, John Boles *(Capt. Herbert Cary)*, Jack Holt *(Col. Robert Morrison)*, Karen Morely *(Mrs. Cary)*, Bill "Bojangles" Robinson *(Uncle Billy)*, Guinn "Big Boy" Williams *(Sergeant Dudley)*, Willie Best *(James Henry)*, Frank McGlynn Sr. *(Abraham Lincoln)*, Bessie Lyle *(Mammy)*, Hannah Washington *(Sally Ann)*, James Flavin *(Guard)*.

The Littlest Rebel: *Bill "Bojangles" Robinson and Shirley Temple*

The Littlest Rebel: *Shirley Temple and Bill "Bojangles" Robinson*

A_s

Shirley Temple vehicles go, *The Littlest Rebel* is one of the best, as the precocious moppet attempts to find her missing father (John Boles), captured by Union troops and falsely accused of spying. The brutality and carnage of the Civil War was definitely avoided as Shirley danced with Bill "Bojangles" Robinson and shared a friendly chat with President Lincoln (Frank McGlynn Sr.), who, with his obviously artificial beard, could have used some help from the makeup department.

Nevertheless, the film was bright entertainment and proved to be a hit with Depression-era audiences. Frank McGlynn Sr. played the role of Lincoln many times, and his appearances as the sixteenth president date back to the early silent era.

The original 1911 play of the same title, by Edward Peple, which was altered considerably for the movie version, had introduced Mary Miles Minter to the stage.

Stepin Fetchit had originally been cast as the "James Henry" character but was replaced by Willie Best when Fetchit developed eye problems because of the intense studio lighting. Charles Bickford had originally been cast in the Jack Holt role but was replaced by Holt when he was mauled by a lion while shooting another film.

Shirley Temple's vocal coach was Jule Styne.

Reviews

"Shirley Temple climbs up on President Lincoln's lap, rescues John Boles from a firing squad and sings a song called 'Polly-Wolly-Doodle.' . . . You may have got the mistaken notion from So Red the Rose *that the War Between the States was filled with ruin, death, rebellious slaves and horrid Yankee barbarians.* The Littlest Rebel *corrects that unhappy thought and presents the conflict as a decidedly chummy little war."*
—NEW YORK TIMES, DECEMBER 20, 1935

"All bitterness and cruelty have been rigorously cut out and the Civil War emerges as a misunderstanding between kindly gentlemen with eminently happy slaves and a cute little girl who sings and dances through the story."
—VARIETY, DECEMBER 25, 1935

SO RED THE ROSE

1935 • Paramount

CREDITS

Producer: Douglas McLean; director: King Vidor; screenplay:
Laurence Stallings, Edwin Justice Mayer, and Maxwell Anderson
(based on the novel by Stark Young); photography: Victor Milner;
music: W. Frank Harling; film editor: Eda Warren; art directors:
Hans Dreier and Ernst Fegte; costumes: Travis Banton.
Running time: 82 minutes.

CAST

Margaret Sullavan *(Vallette Bedford)*, Walter Connolly *(Malcolm
Bedford)*, Janet Beecher *(Sally Bedford)*, Harry Ellerbe *(Edward Bedford)*,
Robert Cummings *(George Pendleton)*, Charles Starrett *(George
McGehee)*, Johnny Downs *(Yankee Boy)*, Daniel Haynes *(William Veal)*,
Randolph Scott *(Duncan Bedford)*, Elizabeth Patterson *(Mary Cherry)*,
Dickie Moore *(Middleton Bedford)*, Clarence Muse *(Cato)*, James Burke
(Major Rushton), Warner Richmond *(Confederate Sergeant)*, Alfred
Delcambre *(Charles Tolliver)*.

So Red the Rose: *Margaret Sullavan*

So Red the Rose: *Werner Richmond, Randolph Scott, and Margaret Sullavan*

Although
the views on slavery voiced in *So Red the Rose* are woefully outdated, the film is interesting in that it depicts the emotional damage wrought on a Southern family by the Civil War one year before the publication of Margaret Mitchell's novel *Gone With the Wind* and four years before producer David O. Selznick's film version. The film at least makes an attempt, however weak, to tackle the political issues of the war and presents a credible romance between Southern belle Margaret Sullavan and her character's cousin, played by Randolph Scott, a man steadfastly opposed to the violence on both sides of the conflict. Although not completely successful, *So Red the Rose* was the best sound-era Civil War film made before *Gone With the Wind.*

Paramount borrowed Margaret Sullavan from Universal for this film, and a few scenes with Sullavan were actually directed by Elizabeth Hill, director King Vidor's wife.

Reportedly, *So Red the Rose* cost $1 million to produce—a big budget for that time.

Some of the Civil War–era antiques on view were supplied by William H. Hazell, who had served in the war.

Reviews

"The cinema goes into well-bred mourning for Stark Young's aristocrats of the old South in the beautifully photographed screen production of So Red the Rose. . . . *It is a well-made sentimental drama, and it celebrates the last days of the planter aristocracy with a warmth, skill and romantic fervor that should delight Mr. Young."*
—*NEW YORK TIMES*, NOVEMBER 28, 1935

"Paramount's filmization of . . . So Red the Rose *is frequently a fine and distinctive cinematic transmutation and almost as often draggy and uncertain. . . . For obvious reasons its south of the Mason-Dixon box-office chances will be superior to the Yank belt."*
—*VARIETY*, DECEMBER 4, 1935

HEARTS IN BONDAGE

1936 • Republic

CREDITS

Producer: Nat Levine; director: Lew Ayres; screenplay: Bernard Shubert, Olive Cooper, and Karl Brown (based on the story by Wallace McDonald); photography: Ernest Miller and Jack Marta; music: Hugo Riesenfeld; film editor: Ralph Dixon; musical director: Harry Grey.
Running time: 72 minutes.

CAST

James Dunn *(Kenneth)*, Mae Clarke *(Constance)*, David Manners *(Raymond)*, Charlotte Henry *(Julie)*, Henry B. Walthall *(Buchanan)*, Fritz Leiber *(Ericsson)*, George Irving *(Commodore Jordan)*, Irving Pichel *(Secretary Welles)*, J. M. Kerrigan *(Paddy)*, Frank McGlynn Sr. *(Abraham Lincoln)*, Ben Alexander *(Eggleston)*, Oscar Apfel *(Captain Gillman)*, Clay Clement *(Worden)*, Edward Gargan *(McPherson)*, Russell Hicks *(Pillsbury)*, George Hayes *(Ezra)*, Douglas Wood *(Farragut)*, Bodil Rosing *(Mrs. Adams)*, Erville Alderson *(Jefferson Davis)*, John Hyams *(Bushnell)*, Etta McDaniels *(Mammy)*, Warner Richmond *(Bucko)*, Lloyd Ingraham *(Timekeeper)*, with Lane Chandler, Hooper Atchley, Smiley Burnette, Eugene Jackson, Earl Aby, Henry Roquemore, Frankie Marvin, Arthur Wanzer, Helen Seaman, Cecil Watson, Maurice Brierre, Clinton Rosemond, and Pat Flaherty.

(Opposite) Hearts in Bondage: *Frank McGlynn Sr. as Abraham Lincoln*

A

hackneyed Civil War–era romantic plot serves as the framework supporting a depiction of the first battle between "ironclad" warships as the USS *Monitor* confronts the CSS *Merrimac*. Directed by Lew Ayres, James Dunn and Mae Clark have the leading roles in this standard period soap opera, enlivened only by the aforementioned battle scenes, filmed with miniatures. Frank McGlynn Sr. once again offers his familiar portrayal of Abraham Lincoln. Primarily an actor, Lew Ayres did direct infrequently, although never with distinction, and his work here is competent but unremarkable.

The *Monitor-Merrimac* battle was depicted again in 1991 in the made-for-cable TV movie *Ironclads*, directed by Delbert Mann and starring Virginia Madsen and Alex Hyde-White.

Review

"*Hearts in Bondage contains some capable artists, a plot that sometimes intrigues, plenty of production and numerous actionful moments. And yet it never jells as a gripping picture except possibly in its naval battle episodes. . . . This will be tabbed as a historical costume picture, and probably the weakest of the current crop. Covering the Civil War period, [the] story centers about the familiar dogfight between the South's* Merrimac *and the North's* Monitor."
—*VARIETY*, OCTOBER 21, 1936

Hearts in Bondage: *James Dunn and Mae Clarke*

The Prisoner of Shark Island: *Warner Baxter*

THE PRISONER OF SHARK ISLAND

1936 • 20th Century–Fox

CREDITS

Producer: Darryl F. Zanuck; director: John Ford; screenplay:
Nunnally Johnson (based on the life of Dr. Samuel A. Mudd); pho-
tography: Bert Glennon; film editor: Jack Murray; musical director:
Louis Silvers; art director: William Darling; set designer: Thomas
Little; costumes: Gwen Wakeling.
Running time: 95 minutes.

CAST

Warner Baxter *(Dr. Samuel A. Mudd)*, Gloria Stuart *(Mrs. Peggy
Mudd)*, Joyce Kay *(Martha Mudd)*, Claude Gillingwater *(Col. Jeremiah
Dyer)*, Douglas Wood *(General Ewing)*, Fred Kohler Jr. *(Sergeant
Cooper)*, Harry Carey *(Commander of Fort Jefferson)*, Paul Fix *(David
Herold)*, John Carradine *(Sergeant Rankin)*, Francis McDonald *(John
Wilkes Booth)*, Arthur Byron *(Mr. Erickson)*, O. P. Heggie *(Dr.
McIntire)*, John McGuire *(Lovett)*, Paul McVey *(Hunter)*, Francis Ford
(Corporal O'Toole), Ernest Whitman *(Buck Tilford)*, Frank Shannon
(Judge Advocate Holt), Frank McGlynn Sr. *(Abraham Lincoln)*, Arthur
Loft *(Carpetbagger)*, Maurice Murphy *(Orderly)*, Paul Stanton *(Orator)*,
Ronald "Jack" Pennick *(Signal Man)*, Merrill McCormick
(Commandant's Aide), James Marcus *(Blacksmith)*, Jan Duggan
(Actress), Lloyd Whitlock *(Major Rathbone)*, Leila McIntyre *(Mrs.
Lincoln)*, Dick Elliott *(Actor)*, Murdock MacQuarrie *(Spangler)*, Bud
Geary, Duke Lee, and Robert E. Homans *(Sergeants)*, Robert Dudley
(Druggist), Wilfred Lucas *(Colonel)*, Cecil Weston *(Mrs. Surratt)*, Cyril
Thornton *(Maurice O'Laughlin)*, Beulah Hall Jones *(Blanche)*, J. M.
Kerrigan *(Judge Maiben)*, Etta McDaniel *(Rosabelle Tiford)*, J. P.
McGowan *(Ship's Captain)*, Harry Strang *(Mate)*, with Whitney
Bourne, Robert Parrish, and Frank Baker.

Warner

Baxter stars as Dr. Samuel A. Mudd, a respected physician who innocently set John Wilkes Booth's leg, which was broken when the actor was injured after assassinating President Lincoln, allowing Booth to go on his way afterward. Mudd was immediately arrested and wrongly vilified as a participant in the assassination conspiracy, then incarcerated at Fort Jefferson on Shark Island. Mudd, separated from his wife (played by Gloria Stuart) and forced to live under harsh prison conditions, eventually performs a heroic act when a yellow-fever epidemic breaks out among the prisoners and, at great risk to himself, saves many lives with his medical skills. Mudd's case is then reopened, and he is exonerated. Although not directly concerned with the Civil War, this true story, tightly directed by John Ford, accurately depicts the "witch-hunt" hysteria following Lincoln's assassination, and Baxter is excellent in the lead.

The same material saw use again in *Hellgate,* a 1952 movie starring Sterling Hayden and directed by Charles Marquis Warren, and in *The Ordeal of Dr. Mudd,* a 1980 made-for-TV movie starring Dennis Weaver and directed by Paul Wendkos.

Reviews

"Fact can be stranger than fiction, and occasionally fiction gets there first. The incredible life story of Dr. Samuel Alexander Mudd, which Twentieth Century–Fox has dramatized in The Prisoner of Shark Island *. . . may be accurate historically, but it still reads like a typical Hollywood scenario."*
—*NEW YORK TIMES,* FEBRUARY 13, 1936

The Prisoner of Shark Island: *Warner Baxter, Gloria Stuart, and Claude Gillingwater*

"*Warner Baxter as Dr. Samuel A. Mudd, 'America's Jean Valjean' of the post–Civil War hysteria, turns in a capital performance as the titular prisoner of 'America's Devil's Island.' It's perhaps his top acting performance.*"
—*VARIETY*, FEBRUARY 19, 1936

"*Excellent film based on [the] true story of Dr. Samuel Mudd. . . . Gripping story; Baxter [is] superb.*"
—LEONARD MALTIN, *LEONARD MALTIN'S TV MOVIES AND VIDEO GUIDE*

Of Human Hearts: *Walter Huston and Beulah Bondi*

OF HUMAN HEARTS

1938 • M-G-M

CREDITS

Producer: John W. Considine Jr.; director: Clarence Brown; screen-
play: Bradbury Foote (based on the story *Benefits Forgot* by Honore
Morrow); photography: Clyde Devinna; music: Herbert Stothart;
film editor: Frank E. Hull; art direction: Cedric Gibbons,
Harry Oliver, and Edwin B. Willis.
Running time: 100 minutes

CAST

Walter Huston *(Ethan Wilkins)*, James Stewart *(Jason Wilkins)*, Beulah
Bondi *(Mary Wilkins)*, Guy Kibbee *(Mr. George Ames)*, Charles
Coburn *(Dr. Charles Shingle)*, John Carradine *(Abraham Lincoln)*, Ann
Rutherford *(Annie Hawks)*, Charley Grapewin *(Mr. Meeker)*, Gene
Lockhart *(Quid)*, Leona Roberts *(Sister Clarke)*, Arthur Ayelsworth
(Mr. Inchpin), Clem Bevans *(Elder Massey)*, Gene Reynolds *(Jason at
Age 12)*, Leatrice Joy Gilbert *(Annie Hawks at Age 10)*, Sterling
Holloway *(Chauncey at Age 18)*, Charles Peck *(Chauncey at Age 12)*,
Robert McWade *(Dr. Crum)*, John Miljan *(Captain Griggs)*, Rosina
Galli *(Mrs. Ardsley)*, Anne O'Neal *(Mrs. Hawks)*, Esther Dale *(Mrs.
Cantwell)*, Brenda Fowler *(Mrs. Ames)*, William Stack *(Salesman)*,
Ward Bond and Frank McGlynn Jr. *(Louts)*, Stanley Fields *(Horse
Owner)*, Roger Moore *(Attendant)*, Guy Bates Post *(Horse Buyer)*, Jack
Mulhall *(Soldier)*, Phillip Terry and Joe Forte *(Interns)*, Morgan
Wallace *(Dr. Crandall)*.

*L*ike

the aforementioned *So Red the Rose, Of Human Hearts* concentrates on the emotional side of the Civil War, with Beulah Bondi, wife of stern patriarch Walter Huston, as the self-sacrificing mother of aspiring doctor James Stewart. Ignored and neglected by her son when he goes off to war, Bondi, unsure of whether Stewart is alive or a battle casualty, writes to President Lincoln (John Carradine) begging for information about her son. Investigating the matter, Lincoln discovers that Stewart is indeed alive and, after sternly reprimanding him, sends the chastened Stewart home to his mother.

Although almost unavoidably mawkish in spots, *Of Human Hearts* was tightly directed by Clarence Brown, and the entire cast was excellent, including an intriguingly cast, effective John Carradine as President Lincoln. The traditional M-G-M production gloss is in full evidence, with excellent photography by Clyde Devinna.

Review

"Frontier life in a village on the banks of the Ohio River in the days preceding the Civil War is the background against which Clarence Brown tells the story of a mother's sacrifice for the career of an ungrateful son. It is an elaborate production, painstaking made. . . ."
—*Variety*, February 9, 1938

Of Human Hearts: *Walter Huston, Beulah Bondi, and James Stewart*

Gone With the Wind: *Clark Gable and Vivien Leigh*

GONE WITH THE WIND

1939 • M-G-M

CREDITS

Producer: David O. Selznick; directors: Victor Fleming (and, uncredited, George Cukor, Sam Wood, William Cameron Menzies, and Sidney Franklin); screenplay: Sidney Howard (and, uncredited, Jo Swerling, Charles MacArthur, Ben Hecht, John Lee Mahin, John Van Druten, Oliver H. P. Garrett, Winston Miller, John Balderston, Michael Foster, Edwin Justus Mayer, F. Scott Fitzgerald, and David O. Selznick; based on the novel by Margaret Mitchell); photography: Ernest Haller and Lee Garmes (Technicolor); music: Max Steiner; musical director: Louis Forbes; film editors: Hal C. Kern and James E. Newcom; production design: William Cameron Menzies; art directors: Lyle Wheeler and Hobe Erwin; set designer: Edward G. Boyle; costumes: Walter Plunkett; special effects: Jack Cosgrove and Lee Zavitz; choreography: Frank Lloyd and Eddie Prinz.
Running time: 220 minutes.

CAST

(in order of appearance)

AT TARA: Fred Crane (*Brent Tarleton*), George Reeves (*Stuart Tarleton*), Vivien Leigh (*Scarlett O'Hara*), Hattie McDaniel (*Mammy*), Everett Brown (*Big Sam*), Zack Williams (*Elijah*), Thomas Mitchell (*Gerold O'Hara*), Oscar Polk (*Pork*), Barbara O'Neill (*Ellen O'Hara*), Victor Jory (*Jonas Wilkerson*), Evelyn Keyes (*Suellen O'Hara*), Ann Rutherford (*Careen O'Hara*), Butterfly McQueen (*Prissy*), Tom Seidel (*Guest*). AT TWELVE OAKS: Howard Hickman (*John Wilkes*), Alicia Rhett (*India Wilkes*), Leslie Howard (*Ashley Wilkes*), Olivia de Havilland (*Melanie Hamilton*), Rand Brooks (*Charles Hamilton*),

Carroll Nye *(Frank Kennedy)*, Marcella Martin *(Cathleen Calvert)*, Clark Gable *(Rhett Butler)*, James Bush *(Gentleman)*, Marjorie Reynolds *(Gossip)*, Ralph Brooks *(Gentleman)*, Philip Trent *(Gentleman—later bearded Confederate on steps at Tara)*. AT THE BAZAAR IN ATLANTA: Laura Hope Crews *(Aunt Pittypat Hamilton)*, Harry Davenport *(Dr. Meade)*, Leona Roberts *(Mrs. Caroline Meade)*, Jane Darwell *(Dolly Merriwether)*, Albert Morin *(René Picard)*, Mary Anderson *(Maybelle Merriwether)*, Terry Shero *(Fanny Elsing)*, William McClain *(Old Levi)*. OUTSIDE THE *EXAMINER* OFFICE: Eddie "Rochester" Anderson *(Uncle Peter)*, Jackie Moran *(Phil Meade)*, Tommy Kelly *(Boy)*. AT THE HOSPITAL: Cliff Edwards *(Reminiscent Soldier)*, Ona Munson *(Bell Watling)*, Ed Chandler *(Sergeant)*, George Hackathorne *(Wounded Soldier)*, Roscoe Ates *(Convalescent Soldier)*, John Arledge *(Dying Soldier)*, Eric Linden *(Amputee)*, Guy Wilkerson *(Wounded Card Player)*. DURING THE EVACUATION: Tom Tyler *(Commanding Officer)*, Frank Faylen *(Soldier Aiding Dr. Meade)*, Junior Coghlan *(Exhausted Boy)*. DURING THE SIEGE: William Bakewell *(Mounted Officer)*, Lee Phelps *(Bartender)*. GEORGIA AFTER SHERMAN: Paul Hurst *(Yankee Deserter)*, Ernest Whitman *(Carpetbagger's Friend)*, William Stelling *(Returning Veteran)*, Louis Jean Heydt *(Hungry Soldier)*, Isabel Jewell *(Emmy Slattery)*, William Stack *(Minister)*. DURING RECONSTRUCTION: Robert Elliott *(Yankee Major)*, George Meeker and Wallace Clark *(His Poker-Playing Captains)*, Irving Bacon *(Corporal)*, Adrian Morris *(Carpetbagger Orator)*, J. M. Kerrigan *(Johnny Gallagher)*, Olin Howland *(Yankee Businessman)*, Yakima Canutt *(Renegade)*, Blue Washington *(His Companion)*, Ward Bond *(Yankee captain Tom)*, Cammie King *(Bonnie Blue Butler)*, Mickey Kuhn *(Beau Wilkes)*, Lillian Kemble Cooper *(Bonnie's Nurse)*, Si Jenks *(Yankee on Street)*, Harry Strang *(Tom's Aide)*, with Emerson Treacy, Trevor Bardette, Lester Dorr, and John Wray.

*I*deally

cast, producer David O. Selznick's oft-screened Technicolor epic *Gone With the Wind* is, simply put, the biggest soap opera ever made. Although Selznick's film is historically accurate in physical detail and broad in its visual extravagance, the film focuses on the *emotional* side of the Civil War and its effects on the characters involved, particularly Southern vixen Scarlett O'Hara (Vivien Leigh). The result is that the entire cast of characters is humanized to a depth and extent that is, unfortunately, rare in period films. This emotional texture, coupled with Selznick's glossy produc-

Gone With the Wind: *Vivien Leigh* (left) *observes Rebel war casualties.*

tion values, has guaranteed the movie's continuing popularity, even more than fifty years after its first release.

Selznick's meticulous attention to costuming and production detail cannot be faulted. Much of the movie's effectiveness can be attributed to the fact that every single shot was storyboarded and preplanned before shooting began. The Technicolor photography, especially when seen in an original 35-mm print, is stunning, and even with all the emotional baggage on hand, there is still plenty of spectacle; the mammoth burning of Atlanta, in particular, is unforgettable. The direction is officially credited to Victor Fleming, but Selznick and production designer William Cameron Menzies are this still-engrossing film's true auteurs.

A 1994 TV miniseries, *Scarlett,* starring Timothy Dalton as Rhett Butler and Joanne Whalley-Kilmer as Scarlett O'Hara, attempted to extend the story but failed to impress either critics or the audience.

Gone With the Wind: *Future TV "Superman" George Reeves (left) and Vivien Leigh*

Reviews

"It is pure narrative, as the novel was, rather than great drama, as the novel was not. . . . You will leave it, not with the feeling you have undergone a profound emotional experience, but with the warm and grateful remembrance of an interesting story beautifully told."
—NEW YORK TIMES, DECEMBER 20, 1939

"After nearly a year of actual filming, editing and scoring, David O. Selznick's production of Gone With the Wind, *from Margaret Mitchell's novel of the Civil War and Reconstruction period, comes to the screen as one of the truly great films. . . . The lavishness of its production, the consummate care and skill which went into its making, the assemblage of its fine cast and expert technical staff combine in presenting a theatrical attraction completely justifying the princely investment of $3,900,000."*
—VARIETY, DECEMBER 20, 1939

"If not the greatest movie ever made, certainly one of the greatest examples of story-telling on film, maintaining interest for over four hours."
—LEONARD MALTIN, LEONARD MALTIN'S TV MOVIES AND VIDEO GUIDE

YOUNG MR. LINCOLN

1939 • 20th Century–Fox

CREDITS

Producer: Kenneth Macgowan; director: John Ford; screenplay:
Lamar Trotti; photography: Bert Glennon and Arthur Miller; music:
Alfred Newman; film editor: Walter Thompson; musical director:
Louis Silvers; art direction: Richard Day and Mark-Lee Kirk; set
designer: Thomas Little; costumes: Royer.
Running time: 100 minutes.

CAST

Henry Fonda (*Abraham Lincoln*), Alice Brady (*Abigail Clay*), Marjorie
Weaver (*Mary Todd*), Arleen Whelan (*Hannah Clay*), Eddie Collins
(*Efe Turner*), Pauline Moore (*Ann Rutledge*), Richard Cromwell (*Matt
Clay*), Ward Bond (*John Palmer Cass*), Donald Meek (*John Felder*),
Spencer Charters (*Judge Herbert A. Bell*), Eddie Quillan (*Adam Clay*),
Dorris Bowdon (*Carrie Sue*), Milburn Stone (*Stephen A. Douglas*), Cliff
Clark (*Sheriff Billings*), Robert Lowery (*Juror*), Charles Tannen (*Ninian
Edwards*), Francis Ford (*Sam Boone*), Fred Kohler Jr. (*Scrub White*),
Kay Linaker (*Mrs. Edwards*), Russell Simpson (*Woodridge*), Edwin
Maxwell (*John T. Stuart*), Charles Halton (*Hawthorne*), Robert
Homans (*Mr. Clay*), Steven Randall (*Juror*), Jack Kelly (*Matt Clay as a
Boy*), Dickie Jones (*Adam Clay as a Boy*), Harry Tyler (*Barber*), Jack
Pennick (*Big Buck*), Louis Mason (*Court Clerk*), Paul Burns, Frank
Orth, George Chandler, and Dave Morris (*Loafers*), Ivar McFadden
(*Juror*), Sylvia McClure (*Baby*), Herbert Heywood (*Official*), Arthur
Aylesworth, Harold Goodwin, Dorothy Vaughan, Virginia Brissac,
Clarence Wilson, and Elizabeth Jones.

Although
not directly concerned with the Civil War, director John Ford's excellent *Young Mr. Lincoln* examines Abraham Lincoln's early years as a struggling lawyer and his defense of a man wrongly accused of murder. Ford's straightforward, unpretentious direction, coupled with star Henry Fonda's engaging performance, emphasizes Lincoln's humble beginnings, revealing his love of books, his passion for learning, and his steadfast morality. Fonda's makeup is especially effective, subtly changing as the film progresses until the star begins to look more "Lincolnesque" toward the conclusion, even donning the familiar stovepipe hat. The result of Ford's careful, restrained direction is a moving, unforgettable portrait of a man soon to be touched by destiny and one of the best films of Ford's and Fonda's careers.

The working titles for the film were *The Young Lincoln, A Younger Lincoln, The Life of Young Abraham Lincoln,* and *Lawyer of the West.*

The film—with Henry Fonda in the lead—had been planned by Fox as early as 1935 but was not filmed at that time because producer Walter Wanger would not sell Fonda's contract to Fox, although he did eventually agree to lend Fonda to the studio for *Young Mr. Lincoln.* At one point before this agreement was reached, Irving Cummings was to have directed, with Tyrone Power cast as Lincoln.

Playwright Robert Sherwood, author of the play *Abe Lincoln in Illinois,* filed a legal complaint against Fox, claiming that their use of the title *Young Mr. Lincoln* would mislead the public into believing that the film was based on his play. However, *Young Mr. Lincoln* screenwriter Lamar Trotti's first draft, entitled *Lincoln Trial Story,* was dated January 7, 1938, and actually predated Sherwood's play. The Sherwood play eventually *was* filmed, by RKO (with Sherwood scripting), as *Abe Lincoln in Illinois* in 1940 and starred Raymond Massey as Lincoln.

The river scenes for *Young Mr. Lincoln* were shot on location around Sacramento, California. The film's final cost was $1,500,000.

Young Mr. Lincoln: *Henry Fonda*

Reviews

"One of John Ford's most memorable films, and not at all the tedious bummer that the title might suggest. The film is an embroidery . . . on an actual murder trial in which Lincoln was the defense lawyer.

Young Mr. Lincoln: *Pauline Moore and Henry Fonda*

Henry Fonda, in one of his best early performances, is funny and poignant as the drawling, awkward young hero. . . ."
—PAULINE KAEL, *5001 NIGHTS AT THE MOVIES*

"One of the most human and humorous of the Lincoln biographies is Young Mr. Lincoln. . . . *Without a touch of self-consciousness or an interlinear hint that its subject is a man of destiny, it has followed Abe through his early years in Illinois. . . . Henry Fonda's characterization is one of those once-in-a-blue-moon things; a crossroads meeting of nature, art and a smart casting director. . . . The result of it, happily, is not merely a natural and straightforward biography, but a film which indisputably has the right to be called Americana."*
—*NEW YORK TIMES*, JUNE 3, 1939

"Zanuck hasn't compromised much with Abraham Lincoln's authenticity as a character, and as a result Henry Fonda's impersonation of Young Mr. Lincoln *is impressively realistic. As the title implies, it deals with the Great Emancipator's early days in Salem, Illinois, emphasizing the Civil War president's then-penchant for inherent honesty, fearlessness, shrewdness, plus such homey qualities as being a champ rail-splitter mixed with an avid hunger for book larnin'."*
—*VARIETY*, JUNE 7, 1939

MORE CIVIL WAR FILMS
OF THE 1930S

Brief
mention should be made of three more Civil War–related films released
during the 1930s. *Judge Priest* (Fox, 1934), a homespun vehicle for rustic
humorist Will Rogers, was not directly related to the war, but it did feature a noteworthy Civil War flashback sequence.

The Three Stooges fought the War Between the States in *Uncivil
Warriors* (Columbia, 1935), a comedy short with the slapstick trio operating as spies behind Confederate lines. An interminable routine in which
the Stooges unknowingly eat pillow feathers while dining and then cough
up the stuffing was notably unamusing. This film was later remade as a
Stooge short, *Uncivil Warbirds* (Columbia, 1946), reusing some scenes from
the earlier version.

Comedy producer Hal Roach's juvenile Our Gang crowd romped
through *General Spanky* (M-G-M, 1937), set during the Civil War. After
hundreds of comedy shorts, this was the first feature the "gang" made,
and the last, after the indifferent reception *General Spanky* received. It's
doubtful that modern audiences would be amused by Buckwheat's portrayal of a young, forlorn slave desperately searching for a master.

Abe Lincoln in Illinois: *Raymond Massey*

ABE LINCOLN IN ILLINOIS

1940 • RKO

CREDITS

Producer: Max Gordon; director: John Cromwell;
screenplay: Robert E. Sherwood (based on his play);
photography: James Wong Howe; music: Roy Webb.
Running time: 110 minutes.

CAST

Raymond Massey *(Abraham Lincoln)*, Gene Lockhart *(Stephen Douglas)*, Ruth Gordon *(Mary Todd Lincoln)*, Mary Howard *(Ann Rutledge)*, Dorothy Tree *(Elizabeth Edwards)*, Harvey Stephens *(Ninian Edwards)*, Minor Watson *(Joshua Speed)*, Alan Baxter *(Billy Herndon)*, Howard da Silva *(Jack Armstrong)*, Maurice Murphy *(John McNeil)*, Clem Bevans *(Ben Battling)*, Herbert Rudley *(Seth Gale)*, Roger Imhof *(Mr. Crimmin)*, Edmund Elton *(Mr. Rutledge)*, George Rosener *(Dr. Chandler)*, Trevor Bardette *(John Hanks)*, Elisabeth Risdon *(Sarah Lincoln)*, Napoleon Simpson *(Gobey)*, Aldrich Bowker *(Judge Bowling Green)*, Louis Jean Heydt *(Mentor Graham)*, Harlan Briggs *(Denton Offut)*, Andy Clyde *(Stage Driver)*, Leona Roberts *(Mrs. Rutledge)*, Florence Roberts *(Mrs. Bowling Green)*, Fay Helm *(Mrs. Seth Gale)*, Syd Saylor *(John Johnston)*, Charles Middleton *(Tom Lincoln)*, Alec Craig *(Trem Cogdall)*.

*A*ware
that director John Ford's *Young Mr. Lincoln* was in production at 20th
Century–Fox, RKO bought the rights to Robert E. Sherwood's successful
stage play about Lincoln, producing this episodic film, with Sherwood
scripting. Although Raymond Massey is excellent as Lincoln, the film's
structure is messy and ill conceived; the picture suffers from many of the
same flaws as D. W. Griffith's 1930 *Abraham Lincoln.*

Although *Abe Lincoln in Illinois* covers more biographical ground
than *Young Mr. Lincoln,* tracing Lincoln's life up to his election in 1860, the
film is less satisfying than Ford's production, and like Griffith's stodgy
Lincoln, Massey is less a human being than a posturing, overblown monument. Sincere and well photographed by the great James Wong Howe,
Abe Lincoln in Illinois was a critical success but failed to click with the
movie-going public, and RKO lost $75,000 on the production.

Not directly concerned with the Civil War, *Abe Lincoln in Illinois* is a
respectable biographical film and, despite its faults, retains interest as a
companion (and comparison) piece to the aforementioned Griffith and
Ford films.

Reviews

*"Lincoln, and the film they have made about him, is a grave and sincere
and moving and eloquent tribute to these United States and to
what they stand for, and must stand for. . . ."*
—*New York Times,* February 23, 1940

*"Human qualities of the Lincoln biography, however, rather than the
historical verity of the picturization, are the likely impelling
factors by which the film will win wide popularity."*
—*Variety,* January 24, 1940

Abe Lincoln in Illinois: *Raymond Massey*

DARK COMMAND

1940 • Republic

CREDITS

Producer: Sol C. Siegel; director: Raoul Walsh; screenplay: Grover
Jones, Lionel Hauser, F. Hugh Herbert, and Jan Fortune (based on
the novel by W. R. Burnett); photography: Jack Marta; film editors:
Murray Seldeen and William Morgan;
art direction: John Victor MacKay.
Running time: 91 minutes.

CAST

John Wayne *(Bob Seton)*, Claire Trevor *(Mary McCloud)*, Walter
Pidgeon *(William Cantrell)*, Roy Rogers *(Fletch McCloud)*, George
"Gabby" Hayes *(Doc Grunch)*, Porter Hall *(Angus McCloud)*, Marjorie
Main *(Mrs. Cantrell)*, Raymond Walburn *(Buckner)*, Joseph Sawyer
(Bushropp), Helen MacKeller *(Mrs. Hale)*, J. Farrell MacDonald
(Dave), Trevor Bardette *(Hale)*, Alan Bridge *(Bandit Leader)*, Ferris
Taylor *(Banker)*, Ernie S. Adams *(Wiry Man)*, Harry Cording *(Killer)*,
Edward Hearn and Edmund Cobb *(Jurymen)*, Glenn Strange *(Tough)*,
Mildred Gover *(Ellie, the Maid)*, Tom London *(Messenger)*, Dick
Alexander *(Sentry)*, Yakima Canutt *(Townsman/Stunts)*, Hal Taliaferro
(Townsman), Jack Rockwell *(Assassin)*, Harry Woods *(Dental Patient)*,
Dick Rich and John Merton *(Cantrell Men)*, with Frank Hagney, John
Dilson, Clinton Rosemund, Budd Buster, Howard Hickman, Al
Taylor, Jack Low, Edward Earle, Joe McGuinn, Harry Strang, Tex
Cooper, Jack Montgomery, Ben Alexander, and Cliff Lyons.

Dark Command: *Claire Trevor*

71

Dark Command: *Claire Trevor, Roy Rogers, and Porter Hall*

*B*ased
on Confederate guerrilla leader William Quantrill's destructive raid on Lawrence, Kansas, during the war, *Dark Command* fabricates a romantic triangle involving John Wayne as a hard-fighting cowhand elected marshal of Lawrence, Southern belle Claire Trevor, and Walter Pidgeon, as Quantrill, here inexplicably renamed Cantrell. The scene involving the burning of Lawrence is big and spectacular; this film was one of the most expensive produced by Republic Pictures at that time, with a budget of $750,000.

Wayne had just hit the big time with the release of John Ford's *Stagecoach* the year before; he and the rest of the cast, under Raoul Walsh's tight direction, are excellent here, and the stunts, performed by Yakima Canutt and other veteran thrill masters, are superb. The story of Quantrill's raid on Lawrence saw service again in *The Woman They Almost Lynched,* a minor 1953 western directed by Allan Dwan, but Quantrill (played by Brian Donlevy) took a backseat to the contrived main plot featuring Joan Leslie as the title figure. The same material was warmed over

to better effect in director Edward Brends's *Quantrill's Raiders* (Columbia, 1958), which is discussed later in this book.

Reviews

"A lot of experience and talent have gone into the manufacture of Republic's Dark Command *. . . and the consequence is the most rousing and colorful horse-opera that has gone thundering past this way since Stagecoach."*
—NEW YORK TIMES, MAY 11, 1940

"The Dark Command *is a lusty and actionful western running to the spectacular in its exposition of pioneer days in Kansas back in the 1860's. It's the highest budgeter for Republic to date, running in [the] neighborhood of $700,000 in negative cost. . . . This one concentrates on the law-abiding citizens of the settlement and the sympathies for the North and South prior to and during the Civil War."*
—VARIETY, APRIL 30, 1940

Dark Command: *John Wayne, Walter Pidgeon, and Claire Trevor*

The Man From Dakota: *Wallace Beery* (right)

THE MAN FROM DAKOTA

1940 • M-G-M

CREDITS

Producer: Edward Chodorov; director: Leslie Fenton; screenplay: Laurence Stallings (based on the novel *Arouse and Beware* by MacKinlay Kantor); photography: Ray June; film editor: Conrad A. Nervig; art direction: Cedric Gibbons and Malcolm Brown; set designer: Edwin B. Willis; costumes: Gile Steele and Dolly Tree; makeup: Jack Dawn.
Running time: 74 minutes.

CAST

Wallace Beery *(Sergeant Barstow)*, John Howard *(Oliver Clark)*, Dolores Del Rio *(Eugenia, "Jenny")*, Donald Meek *(Mr. Vestry)*, Robert Barrat *(Parson Summers)*, Addison Richards *(Provost Marshal)*, Frederick Burton *(Leader)*, John Wray *(Carpenter)*, Gregory Gaye *(Colonel Borodin)*, Frank Hagney *(Guard)*, William Royle *(Supervisor)*, Ted Oliver and Buddy Roosevelt *(Officers)*, Hugh Sothern *(General)*, Edward Hearn *(Captain)*, John Butler *(Voss)*, Tom Fadden *(Driver)*, Francis Ford *(Horseman)*, William Haade *(Union Soldier)*.

Wallace

Beery and John Howard star as Union officers who escape from a Confederate prison and make their way back to Northern lines, becoming involved with a beautiful Russian immigrant (played by Dolores Del Rio) along the way. Del Rio has killed a Confederate officer; Beery and Howard recover from the body a map detailing enemy positions and eventually turn it in to General Grant, thereby aiding the Union cause.

The best thing about this contrived M-G-M Wallace Beery vehicle was Ray June's excellent photography. This film is also known by the title of the MacKinlay Kantor novel on which it is based, *Arouse and Beware*. According to the late John Howard, M-G-M star Robert Taylor was originally slated to play Howard's role but declined, believing the film was not a prestigious enough vehicle.

Reviews

"As Beery comedy, **The Man From Dakota** *is probably only half-bad, although we don't mind confessing that we no longer roll in the aisles when Mr. B takes a hitch in his belt, tucks his shirt-tail in and cleverly growls 'Awww!' As a version of Mr. Kantor's* Arouse and Beware, *it is so inept we wonder why Metro bought the screen rights in the first place."*
—*NEW YORK TIMES,* FEBRUARY 22, 1940

"The film version of MacKinlay Kantor's adventure story of two escaping Union soldiers, who weave through the Confederate lines to ultimately save Grant's forces from disaster, falls short of the dramatic suspense and sustained interest displayed on the printed pages."
—*VARIETY,* FEBRUARY 21, 1940

The Man From Dakota: *John Howard, Dolores Del Rio, and Wallace Beery*

Santa Fe Trail: *Ronald Reagan and Errol Flynn*

SANTA FE TRAIL

1940 • Warner Bros.

CREDITS
Producers: Jack L. Warner and Hal B. Wallis; director: Michael
Curtiz; screenplay: Robert Buckner; photography: Sol Polito; music:
Max Steiner; film editor: George Amy; art direction: John Hughes;
costumes: Milo Anderson; special effects: Byron Haskin and H. F.
Koenekamp; makeup: Perc Westmore.
Running time: 110 minutes.

CAST
Errol Flynn *(Jeb Stuart)*, Olivia de Havilland *(Kit Carson Halliday)*,
Raymond Massey *(John Brown)*, Ronald Reagan *(George Armstrong
Custer)*, Alan Hale *(Barefoot Brody)*, Guinn "Big Boy" Williams *(Tex
Bell)*, Van Heflin *(Rader)*, Henry O'Neill *(Cyrus Halliday)*, William
Lundigan *(Bob Halliday)*, John Litel *(Harlan)*, Gene Reynolds *(Jason
Brown)*, Alan Baxter *(Oliver Brown)*, Moroni Olsen *(Robert E. Lee)*,
Erville Alderson *(Jefferson Davis)*, Suzanne Carnahan, "Susan Peters"
(Charlotte Davis), Charles D. Brown *(Major Sumner)*, David Bruce
(Phil Sheridan), Frank Wilcox *(James Longstreet)*, William Marshall
(George Pickett), George Haywood *(John Hood)*, Russell Simpson
(Shoubel Morgan), Joseph Sawyer *(Kitzmiller)*, Hobart Cavanaugh
(Barber Doyle), Spencer Charters *(Conductor)*, Ward Bond *(Townley)*,
Wilfred Lucas *(Weiner)*, Charles Middleton *(Gentry)*, Russell Hicks *(J.
Boyce Russell)*, Napoleon Simpson *(Samson)*, Cliff Clark *(Instructor)*,
Harry Strang *(Sergeant)*, Emmett Vogan *(Lieutenant)*, Selmer Jackson,
Joseph Crehan, and William Hopper *(Officers)*, Clinton Rosemond,

Bernice Pilot, Libby Taylor, and Mildred Gover *(Blacks)*, Roy Barcroft and Frank Mayo *(Engineers)*, Grace Stafford *(Farmer's Wife)*, Louis Jean Heydt *(Farmer)*, Lane Chandler *(Adjutant)*, Richard Kipling *(Army Doctor)*, Jack Mower *(Surveyor)*, Trevor Bardette and Nestor Paiva *(Agitators)*, Mira McKinney, Harry Cording, James Farley, Alan Bridge, Eddy Waller, and John Meyer *(Workman)*, Maris Wrixon, Lucia Carroll, and Mildred Coles *(Girls)*, Georgia Caine *(Officer's Wife)*, Arthur Aylesworth, Walter Soldering, and Henry Hall *(Abolitionists)*, Theresa Harris *(Maid)*, Jess Lee Brooks *(Doorman)*, Eddy Chandler, Edmund Cobb, Ed Peil, and Ed Hearn *(Guards)*, Victor Kilian *(Dispatch Rider)*, Creighton Hale *(Telegraph Operator)*, Alec Proper *(Townsman)*, Rev. Neal Dodd and Lafe McKee *(Ministers)*, Addison Richards *(Sheriff)*.

Regrettably inaccurate as history, with a blurred moral point of view as well, *Santa Fe Trail* is nevertheless directed with high energy by Michael Curtiz. Although the film's story predates the Civil War, it portrays several key Civil War–era figures, including "Jeb" Stuart (Flynn), George Armstrong Custer (Ronald Reagan), Phil Sheridan (David Bruce), James Longstreet (Frank Wilcox), and George Pickett (William Marshall), all erroneously shown attending West Point at the same time.

With Olivia de Havilland tossed in as romantic interest, the principals soon team up to defeat abolitionist John Brown, portrayed here in a flurry of bulging eyes and fanatical oratory by an enjoyable hammy Raymond Massey. Worthless as history, *Santa Fe Trail* stumbles as entertainment as well. Is John Brown a good guy or a bad guy? Or simply misguided? Apparently, no one connected with the production of this film could hazard a guess, and this is where the picture fails and collapses into a morally ambiguous mess.

Curtiz was one of the best studio directors working during Hollywood's golden age, but he is nearly defeated here by a lopsided script marred by too much studio interference.

The working title for this film was *Diary of the Santa Fe. Santa Fe Trail* was shot on location around Santa Fe, New Mexico.

Reviews

"The judgment of history upon John Brown is divided, it is true. Some hold that he was a great martyr to the cause of freeing the slaves; others suspect he was just a wild fanatic driven mad by a high ideal. . . . Still, the story demanded a bad man for Mr. Flynn and his laddies to chase, so John Brown turns out it."
—NEW YORK TIMES, DECEMBER 21, 1940

"Director Curtiz and Robert Buckner, original scripter, smartly never permit the John Brown character to dominate. . . . Errol Flynn again measures up to his heroic assignment."
—VARIETY, DECEMBER 19, 1940

"One of Hollywood's careless, shameless distortions of American history. The team of Errol Flynn and Olivia de Havilland had thrived under the direction of Michael Curtiz in such films as Captain Blood, The Adventures of Robin Hood, *and* Dodge City, *and so this bloated Western was confected. Flynn plays a monolithically brave Jeb Stuart, and Ronald Reagan is young George Armstrong Custer. . . . The offensive plot pits the two handsome young blades . . . against a rabid, fanatic John Brown (Raymond Massey, at his most burning-eyed hypertense peak and photographed to inspire fear and revulsion in the audience). The black men whom Brown seeks to liberate appear to be childish dupes. It's a romantic, action-filled, screwed-up epic. . . ."*
—PAULINE KAEL, 5001 NIGHTS AT THE MOVIES

(Top) Virginia City: *Randolph Scott, Errol Flynn, and Miriam Hopkins*
(Bottom) Randolph Scott and Humphrey Bogart

VIRGINIA CITY

1940 • Warner Bros.

CREDITS

Producer: Robert Fellows; director: Michael Curtiz; screenplay:
Robert Buckner and, uncredited, Norman Reilly Raine and Howard
Koch; photography: Sol Polito; music: Max Steiner; film editor:
George Amy; art direction: Ted Smith; special effects: Byron Haskin
and H. F. Koenekamp; makeup: Perc Westmore.
Running time: 121 minutes.

CAST

Errol Flynn *(Kerry Bradford)*, Miriam Hopkins *(Julia Hayne)*,
Randolph Scott *(Vance Irby)*, Humphrey Bogart *(John Murrell)*, Frank
McHugh *(Mr. Upjohn)*, Alan Hale *(Olaf "Moose" Swenson)*, Guinn
"Big Boy" Williams *("Marblehead")*, John Litel *(Marshall)*, Moroni
Olsen *(Dr. Cameron)*, Russell Hicks *(Armistead)*, Douglas Dumbrille
(Major Drewery), Dickie Jones *(Cobby)*, Monte Montague, Bud
Osborne *(Stage Drivers)*, Lane Chandler *(Soldier Clerk)*, Trevor
Bardette *(Fanatic)*, Frank Wilcox and Ed Keene *(Officers)*, George
Regas *(Half-Breed)*, Russell Simpson *(Gayford)*, Thurston Hall *(General
Meade)*, Charles Middleton *(Jefferson Davis)*, Victor Kilian *(Abraham
Lincoln)*, Charles Trowbridge *(Seddon)*, Howard Hickman *(General
Page)*, Charles Halton *(Ralston)*, Roy Gordon *(Major General Taylor)*,
Ward Bond *(Sergeant Sam McDaniel)*, Spencer Charters, George Guhl
(Bartenders), Ed Parker and DeWolfe Hopper *(Lieutenants)*, Paul Fix
(Murrell's Henchman), Walter Miller and Reed Howes *(Sergeants)*,
George Reeves *(Telegrapher)*, Wilfred Lucas *(Southerner)*, Brandon
Tynan *(Trenholm)*, Tom Dugan *(Spieler)*, Harry Cording *(Scarecrow)*.

A

quasi-sequel to Errol Flynn's previous Warner Bros. vehicle *Dodge City* (1939), *Virginia City* stars Flynn as a Union officer who, escaping from a Confederate prison, tries to prevent a $5 million gold shipment from reaching the Confederacy. Traveling to the title city, Flynn is pitted against Randolph Scott (who commanded the prison Flynn had escaped from) and Humphrey Bogart (hilariously miscast as a Mexican bandit) in the process and still finds time to romance Confederate spy Miriam Hopkins, who is moonlighting as a dance-hall girl!

Virginia City was directed by Michael Curtiz, who had also helmed *Dodge City*, and, as in *Santa Fe Trail*, Curtiz is stymied by a half-baked script. After the exciting opening scene depicting Flynn's escape from prison, the film never quite regains momentum. The aforementioned miscasting is also a problem, both with Bogart and Miriam Hopkins. The fortyish Hopkins, a leading lady of the early 1930s, was definitely past her prime here, and her romantic scenes with Flynn are simply not believable.

Virginia City was shot on location at Sherwood Lake, California; Victorville, California; and on the Painted Desert, Arizona.

Errol Flynn and Martha Scott starred in a *Lux Radio Theatre* version of the film, broadcast on May 26, 1941.

Reviews

"As a shoot 'em up, the picture is first class; as a bit of cinematic history telling, it is far short of the possibilities indicated by the title and cast. . . . Michael Curtiz, the director, has taken all this and steamed it up with some noisy trigger work, charging cavalry, dance-hall intimacies and the burning sands of the desert to concoct a bustling western, which is replete with action, although short on credulity."
—VARIETY, MARCH 20, 1940

Virginia City: *Errol Flynn and Randolph Scott*

"Follow-up to Dodge City *has big cast in lush Civil War Western, but tale of rebel spy Hopkins posing as dance-hall girl doesn't live up to expectations."*
—LEONARD MALTIN, *LEONARD MALTIN'S TV MOVIES AND VIDEO GUIDE*

Belle Starr: *Gene Tierney*

BELLE STARR

1941 • 20th Century–Fox

CREDITS

Producer: Kenneth Macgowan; director: Irving Cummings; screenplay: Lamar Trotti (based on a story by Niven Busch and Cameron Rogers); photography: Ernest Palmer and Ray Rennahan (Technicolor); music: Alfred Newman; film editor: Robert Simpson. Running time: 87 minutes.

CAST

Randolph Scott *(Sam Starr)*, Gene Tierney *(Belle Starr)*, Dana Andrews *(Major Thomas Crall)*, John Sheppard, "Shepperd Strudwick" *(Ed Shirley)*, Elizabeth Patterson *(Sarah)*, Chill Wills *(Blue Duck)*, Louise Beavers *(Mammy Lou)*, Olin Howland *(Jasper Trench)*, Paul Burns *(Sergeant)*, Joseph Sawyer *(John Cole)*, Joseph Downing *(Jim Cole)*, Howard Hickman *(Colonel Thornton)*, Charles Trowbridge *(Colonel Bright)*, James Flavin *(Sergeant)*, Charles Middleton *(Carpetbagger)*.

Wildly

inaccurate historically, *Belle Starr* grossly misrepresents the notorious female bandit and prostitute in the form of Gene Tierney, who plays Starr as a genteel, somewhat misunderstood Southern belle á la Scarlett O'Hara (Tierney even uses a Southern accent like Vivien Leigh's). She teams with Randolph Scott (as her husband, Sam Starr) to fight on in the "lost cause" of the Confederacy. A romantic triangle is fabricated in the process, with Dana Andrews as a Union officer who also loves Belle.

It should be noted that the real Belle Starr never fought for any cause in the Civil War and was a common thief who only stole for her own ends; nor was she nearly as attractive as Gene Tierney. Twentieth Century–Fox studio head Darryl F. Zanuck was obviously influenced by the massive success of *Gone With the Wind* in the production of this glossy confection, which is more successful as entertainment than as history.

Betty Compson had also played Belle Starr in the silent film *Court-Martial* (Columbia, 1928), starring Jack Holt, and Elizabeth Montgomery played Belle in *Belle Starr,* a 1980 made-for-TV movie that was a bit more accurate than the Tierney film but still historically dubious. A sequel to the Tierney picture, *Belle Starr's Daughter,* was released in 1948, with Ruth Roman in the title role.

Reviews

"To the panel of neurotic unreconstructed rebels spawned in the aftermath of the Civil War, Twentieth Century–Fox has added the portrait of a gun-toting lady in Belle Starr. . . . *As has become almost habitual by now in films of post-war desperadoes, Hollywood has turned the tables on history. Instead of a female thug she turns out to be a sort of border Joan of Arc fighting bravely for the lost cause of the Confederacy."*
—*NEW YORK TIMES, NOVEMBER 1, 1941*

Belle Starr: *Randolph Scott and Gene Tierney*

"Twentieth–Fox makes a good job of completely botching up the
historical character it pretends to portray. This is a weak-kneed
and thoroughlyfalse biography of the Southwest's most notorious
female bandit . . . who is dressed up instead as a Missouri slave-
owning aristocrat devoting her very life to fighting
the 'damn Yankees.'"
—*Variety*, August 27, 1941

A Southern Yankee: *Brian Donlevy and John Ireland*

A SOUTHERN YANKEE

1948 • M-G-M

CREDITS

Producer: Paul Jones; director: Edward Sedgwick; screenplay: Harry
Tugend (based on a story by Melvin Frank and Norman Panama);
photography: Ray June; music: David Snell; film editor: Ben Lewis;
art direction: Cedric Gibbons and Randall Duell; set designers:
Edwin B. Willis and Arthur Krams; costumes: Valles; special effects:
Warren Newcombe; makeup: Jack Dawn.
Running time: 90 minutes.

CAST

Red Skelton *(Aubrey Filmore)*, Brian Donlevy *(Curt Devlynn)*, Arlene
Dahl *(Sallyann Weatharby)*, George Coulouris *(Major Jack Drumman)*,
Lloyd Gough *(Captain Steve Lorford)*, John Ireland *(Captain Jed
Calbern)*, Minor Watson *(General Watkins)*, Charles Dingle *(Colonel
Weatharby)*, Art Baker *(Colonel Clifford M. Baker)*, Reed Hadley *(Fred
Munsey)*, Arthur Space *(Mark Haskins)*, Addison Richards *(Dr.
Clayton)*, Joyce Compton *(Hortense Dobson)*, Paul Harvey *(Mr.
Twitchell)*, Jeff Corey *(Union Cavalry Sergeant)*, Cliff Clark *(Dr. Cooper)*,
Dick Wessel, Ian MacDonald, and John Hilton *(Orderlies)*, Ed Gargan
(Male Nurse), David Sharpe *(Confederate Officer)*, Frank McGrath
(Dispatch Rider), David Newell *(Sentry)*, William Tannen, Stanley
Andrews, Roger Moore, and Dick Simmons *(Secret Service Men)*,
Susan Simon *(Jenny)*, Byron Foulger *(Mr. Duncan)*, Paul Newlan
(Man with Saber), Howard Mitchell, Paul Krueger, Vic Zimmerman,
Chris Frank, and James Logan *(Men)*, Marcus Turk, Ralph

Montgomery ,and Walter Merrill *(Confederate Soldiers)*, Ralph Volkie,
Steve Bennett, Allen Mathews, and William "Bill" Phillips *(Soldiers)*,
Ann Staunton *(Nurse)*, Henry Hall *(Thadeus Drumman)*, Lane
Chandler and Carl Saxe *(Sentries)*, Weldon Heyburn, Sam Flint, Jack
Lee, and Forbes Murray *(Officers)*, Harry Cording, Kermit Maynard,
John Merton, and Frank Hagney *(Horsemen)*, Shelly Bacon and
Drexle Bobbie Haywood *(Boys)*, Dick Alexander *(Bartender)*, Rod
O'Connor *(Major Kingsby)*, Pierre Watkin *(Major)*, Bert Moorehouse
(Captain Jeffrys), Bill Kennedy *(Lieutenant Sheve)*.

*I*n
this comedy, lavishly produced by M-G-M, Red Skelton stars as a moronic
bellhop at a St. Louis, Missouri, hotel during the Civil War. Eventually, he
is recruited to impersonate a notorious Confederate spy, the Gray Spider,
behind enemy lines. While aiding the Union cause, Skelton finds time to
romance Arlene Dahl in this hit-and-miss effort, which does have its
worthwhile moments.

Whatever comedic gold there is to be found here is due to the efforts
of two men—Skelton, a genuinely talented comic when supported by
good material, and former silent-screen great Buster Keaton, then down
on his luck and working for Metro as an unbilled gagman. Keaton saw
untapped greatness in Skelton and unsuccessfully attempted to persuade
M-G-M studio head Louis B. Mayer to let them team up for a series of
comedies. Although Mayer turned down Keaton's offer, he did assign him
to devise gags for *A Southern Yankee,* and the film's best visual moments
are due to Keaton's ingenuity, prompting the viewer to wish that he had
been allowed to direct the film!

Reviews

*"That Mr. Skelton is unable to accomplish anything with the material
handed him . . . is not his fault. He's a natural comic with a flexible face
and a likable personality. . . . There may be some farcical merit in the idea
of a simpleton bellhop in a St. Louis hotel masquerading as a fabulous*

A Southern Yankee: *Red Skelton* (left) *and George Coulouris*

Confederate spy and going behind the lines to contact a Union
army agent, but it doesn't come through on the screen."
—*NEW YORK TIMES*, NOVEMBER 25, 1948

"About the only sense A Southern Yankee *makes is that it has Red*
Skelton. That's enough. It's as wild and raucous a conglomeration
of gags as Skelton's recent The Fuller Brush Man.*"*
—*VARIETY*, AUGUST 11, 1948

TAP ROOTS

1948 • Universal-International

CREDITS

Producer: Walter Wanger; director: George Marshall; screenplay: Alan LeMay and Lionel Wiggam (based on the novel by James Street); photography: Lionel Linon and Winton C. Hoch (Technicolor); music: Frank Skinner; production designer: Alexander Golitzen; art direction: Frank A. Richards; set designers: Russell A. Gausman and Ruby R. Levitt; costumes: Yvonne Wood; makeup: Bud Westmore.
Running time: 109 minutes.

CAST

Van Heflin *(Keith Alexander)*, Susan Hayward *(Morna Dabney)*, Boris Karloff *(Tishomingo)*, Julie London *(Aven Dabney)*, Whitfield Connor *(Clay MacIvor)*, Ward Bond *(Hoab Dabney)*, Richard Long *(Bruce Dabney)*, Arthur Shields *(Reverend Kirkland)*, Griff Barnett *(Dr. MacIntosh)*, Sondra Rodgers *(Shellie)*, Ruby Dandridge *(Dabby)*, Russell Simpson *(Sam Dabney)*, Jack Davis *(Militia Captain)*, Gregg Barton *(Captain)*, George Hamilton *(Quint)*, Jonathan Hale *(General Johnston)*, Arthur Space and Kay Medford *(Callers)*, William Haade *(Mob Leader)*, Harry Cording *(Leader)*, Bill Neff and Keith Richards *(Lieutenants)*, Dick Dickinson *(Field Hand)*, Elmo Lincoln *(Sergeant)*, with George Lewis, Helen Mowery, William Challee, John James, and Hank Worden.

(Opposite) Tap Roots: *Van Heflin, Susan Hayward, and Whitfield Connor*

*I*n

Tap Roots, Ward Bond plays the leader of a Lebanon Valley, Mississippi, community determined to remain neutral during the Civil War. When Mississippi secedes from the Union, Lebanon Valley withdraws from Mississippi, with the locals solidly backing the cause of neutrality. Confederate troops invade the valley but, repulsed by a violent counterattack, eventually decide to respect the inhabitants' desires.

Susan Hayward is on hand as a fiery Southern woman cast from the same mold as Scarlett O'Hara in *Gone With the Wind*—a role Hayward had desired but was denied and in effect plays here, and very well. Horror-movie star Boris Karloff plays a supporting role as a friendly Indian; Karloff had also played an Indian the previous year in Cecil B. DeMille's *Unconquered.*

Although well mounted and lavishly shot in Technicolor, *Tap Roots* was too derivative of *Gone With the Wind* and was not successful with the public.

Reviews

"History tells us that the Confederate army had to divert some of its troops to put down a rebellious community in Mississippi which declared itself neutral and independent of state rule. That much of Tap Roots *can be justified, but the manner in which the incident has been embellished for dramatic purposes is something else again. . . . The weaknesses of* Tap Roots *are obvious. The script is a conglomeration of clichés, oral and visual, and none of the characters possess individuality or substance."*
—NEW YORK TIMES, AUGUST 26, 1948

"The George Marshall production . . . spins a fact-fiction tale of a Mississippi Valley family that tried to stand against the South and the North at the beginning of the War Between the States. Marshall's direction points up the pulp-fiction quality of the narrative, giving sweep to the mass-action battle scenes."
—VARIETY, JUNE 30, 1948

Tap Roots: *Susan Hayward*

97

⚔

THE REDHEAD AND THE COWBOY

1950 • Paramount

CREDITS

Producer: Irving Asher; director: Leslie Fenton; screenplay: Jonathan
Latimer and Liam O'Brien (based on the story by Charles Marquis
Warren); photography: Daniel L. Fapp; music: David Buttolph; film
editor: Arthur Schmidt; art direction: Hal Pereira and
Henry Bumstead.
Running time: 82 minutes.

CAST

Glenn Ford *(Gil Kyle)*, Edmund O'Brien *(Dunn Jeffers)*, Rhonda
Fleming *(Candace Bronson)*, Alan Reed *(Lamartine)*, Morris Ankrum
(Sheriff), Edith Evanson *(Mrs. Barrett)*, Perry Ivins *(Mr. Barrett)*,
Janine Perreau *(Mary Barrett)*, Douglas Spencer *(Perry)*, Ray Teal
(Brock), Ralph Byrd *(Captain Andrews)*, King Donovan *(Munroe)*,
Tom Moore *(Gus)*.

(Opposite) The Redhead and the Cowboy: *Glenn Ford and Rhonda Fleming*

*T*he *Redhead and the Cowboy* was a convoluted and lighthearted Civil War spy caper involving a shipment of Union gold sought by Confederates, the story taking place during the closing days of the war. Glenn Ford, Rhonda Fleming, and especially Edmund O'Brien give excellent performances. This was the final movie directed by Leslie Fenton, who retired after a thirty-year career as both a director and actor. Glenn Ford had played a returning Civil War vet in a previous film, *The Man From Colorado* (Columbia, 1948), a minor western costarring William Holden.

Reviews

"It's a tight-reined Western spy film, stuffed with murders and mystery, ending up with a wagon-train gun fight, and not bad, as such roughage goes."
—NEW YORK TIMES, JUNE 6, 1951

"Story has a tight-lipped unfoldment, the terseness being carried to the point of obscurity as both characters and audience are kept in the dark by the step-by-step development. However, [its] method of telling generates suspense, and had not its plot fallen apart near its climactic stage, [the] overall effect would have been good."
—VARIETY, DECEMBER 13, 1950

The Redhead and the Cowboy: *Rhonda Fleming and Glenn Ford*

101

Rocky Mountain: *Errol Flynn*

ROCKY MOUNTAIN

1950 • Warner Bros.

CREDITS

Producer: William Jacobs; director: William Keighley; screenplay:
Alan LeMay and Winston Miller (based on the story "Ghost
Mountain" by LeMay); photography: Ted McCord; music: Max
Steiner; film editor: Rudi Fehr; art direction: Stanley Fleischer; set
designer: L. S. Edwards; costumes: Marjorie Best.
Running time: 83 minutes.

CAST

Errol Flynn *(Lafe Barstow)*, Patrice Wymore *(Johanna Carter)*, Scott
Forbes *(Lieutenant Rickey)*, Guinn "Big Boy" Williams *(Pap Dennison)*,
Dick Jones *(Jim Wheat)*, Howard Petrie *(Cole Smith)*, Slim Pickens
(Plank), Chubby Johnson *(Gil Craigie)*, Buzz Henry *(Kip Waterson)*,
Sheb Wooley *(Kay Rawlins)*, Peter Coe *(Pierre Duchesne)*, Rush
Williams *(Jonas Weatherby)*, Steve Dunhill *(Ash)*, Alex Sharp *(Barnes)*,
Yakima Canutt *(Ryan)*, Nakai Snez *(Man Dog)*.

*I*n

this well-directed but uneventful western, Errol Flynn stars as a Confederate agent intent on gaining a section of western territory in the name of the Confederacy. Punctuated by exciting action scenes, the film is otherwise thin and uneventful and marked Flynn's last appearance in a western. Flynn, still a capable performer and a box-office draw, was nevertheless obviously past his prime by this point and would live only another nine years. Upon its original release, *Rocky Mountain* generated public interest not for the film itself but as a result of Flynn's offscreen romance with costar Patrice Wymore.

Reviews

"Errol Flynn is an ever gallant fellow, but he seems to carry gallantry too far in Warner Brothers' Rocky Mountain. . . . *So far, in fact, does he carry it in guiding a beautiful dame from a horde of ravaging Indians that he ends up as full of arrows as a war-bonnet is full of feathers."*
—NEW YORK TIMES, NOVEMBER 4, 1950

"Warners is giving Rocky Mountain *a fast push into | the market to take advantage of the romantic news involving its star, Errol Flynn, and leading lady, Patrice Wymore. . . . Flynn's role is unusual for him. He's a hero but doesn't get the girl and winds up dead at the finale. However, his performance pleases and helps to sustain interest."*
—VARIETY, OCTOBER 4, 1950

Rocky Mountain: *Errol Flynn, Patrice Wymore, and Howard Petrie*

DRUMS IN THE DEEP SOUTH

1951 • RKO

CREDITS

Producers: Maurice King and Frank King; director: William
Cameron Menzies; screenplay: Philip Yordan and Sidney Harmon
(based on a story by Hollister Noble); photography: Lionel Linden
(Supercinecolor); music: Dimitri Tiomkin; film editor: Richard
Heermance; art direction: William Cameron Menzies.
Running time: 87 minutes.

CAST

James Craig *(Clay)*, Barbara Payton *(Kathy)*, Guy Madison *(Will
Deering)*, Barton MacLane *(McCardle)*, Craig Stevens *(Braxton
Summers)*, Tom Fadden *(Purdy)*, Robert Osterloh *(Harper)*, Taylor
Holmes *(Albert Monroe)*, Robert Easton *(Jerry)*, Lewis Martin *(General
Johnston)*, Peter Brocco *(Union Corporal)*, Dan White *(Corporal
Jennings)*, Louis Jean Heydt *(Colonel House)*.

(Opposite) Drums in the Deep South: *James Craig and Barbara Payton*

*I*n
Drums in the Deep South, Guy Madison, James Craig, and Craig Stevens star as three graduating West Pointers who are drawn into the Civil War as it begins, Madison fighting for the Union cause, Craig and Stevens for the Confederacy. Craig's wife, played by Barbara Payton, doubles as a Confederate agent, spying on Madison and the Union troops and passing information on to her husband. Hampered by a contrived script, *Drums in*

Drums in the Deep South: *James Craig, Lewis Martin, Harry Lewis, and Roy Gordon*

the *Deep South* retains some interest due to the visual flourishes provided by director William Cameron Menzies, the brilliant production designer of *Gone With the Wind.*

Drums in the Deep South, filmed in Supercinecolor, is a better-than-average film largely because of Menzies's efforts, but most of the public attention garnered by the film in 1951 was due to its scandalous leading lady, Barbara Payton. Involved in well-publicized affairs with actors Franchot Tone and Tom Neal, Payton was eventually arrested for prostitution and check forgery, her Hollywood career ruined.

Reviews

*"The . . . screenplay . . . is somewhat confused in the opening
scenes. Characters are not sufficiently established, and it is
not until the closing reels that identities of several of the principals
are clearly defined. There also seems to be an indecision as to
whether to point up the romantic values or the action. Ex–West
Point roommates Guy Madison, James Craig, and Craig Stevens
are holding a reunion at the latter's Georgia home when the
Civil War breaks out. . . . William Cameron Menzies's direction
tends to drag except in some stirring sequences depicting
the struggle to mount the guns on the bluff and the subsequent
shelling of supply trains."*
—VARIETY, OCTOBER 3, 1951

*"Stagnant Civil War yarn of West Pointers
who find themselves fighting
for opposite causes."*
—LEONARD MALTIN, *LEONARD MALTIN'S TV MOVIES AND VIDEO GUIDE*

The Red Badge of Courage: *Audie Murphy and John Dierkes*

THE RED BADGE OF COURAGE

1951 • M-G-M

CREDITS

Producer: Gottfried Reinhardt; director: John Huston; screenplay:
John Huston (based on the novel by Stephen Crane, adapted by
Albert Band); photography: Harold Rosson; music: Bronislau Kaper;
film editor: Ben Lewis; art direction: Cedric Gibbons
and Hans Peters.
Running time: 69 minutes.

CAST

Audie Murphy *(Henry Fleming the Youth)*, Bill Mauldin *(Tom Wilson
the Loud Soldier)*, Douglas Dick *(Lieutenant)*, Royal Dano *(Tattered
Man)*, John Dierkes *(Jim Conlin the Tall Soldier)*, Arthur Hunnicutt
(Bill Porter), Andy Devine *(Fat Soldier)*, Robert Easton Burke
(Thompson), Smith Ballew *(Captain)*, Glenn Strange *(Colonel)*, Dan
White *(Sergeant)*, Frank McGraw *(Captain)*, Tim Durant *(General)*,
Emmett Lynn, Stanford Jolley, William "Bill" Phillips, House Peters
Jr., and Frank Sully *(Veterans)*, George Offerman Jr., Joel Marston,
and Robert Nichols *(Union Soldiers)*, Lou Nova, Fred Kohler Jr., Dick
Curtis, Guy Wilkerson, and Buddy Roosevelt *(Veterans)*, Jim
Hayward *(Soldier)*, Gloria Eaton *(Southern Girl)*, Robert Cherry
(Soldier Who Sings), Whit Bissel *(Wounded Officer)*, William Phipps
(Officer), Ed Hinton *(Corporal)*, Lynn Farr *(Confederate)*,
James Whitmore *(Voice)*.

*P*roduced

at a cost of $1,600,000, director John Huston's *Red Badge of Courage* is one of the finest movies ever released on the Civil War, or for that matter, war in general, examining the thin line between heroism and cowardice—something most war films never do. Like author Stephen Crane, who wrote the original novel from his study of Matthew Brady's Civil War photographs, Huston studied those same photographs in preparing to make the film. The result is stunning pictorial verisimilitude rarely achieved on-screen, made all the more powerful by the tightly controlled performances, especially Audie Murphy's in the role of young Henry Fleming. Murphy was the most decorated hero of World War II, and *The Red Badge of Courage* is his best film.

Running only sixty-nine minutes, *The Red Badge of Courage* was, unfortunately cut by M-G-M after Huston completed it, and the studio, unsure of the picture's commercial viability, hurriedly released it as the bottom half of a double bill. Huston's original cut is said to have run at least nine minutes longer, and the director always maintained that if it hadn't been for M-G-M's editorial meddling, *The Red Badge of Courage* would have been his best film. What remains, however, is still excellent and highly recommended.

The Stephen Crane novel was filmed again, in 1974, as a made-for-TV movie starring Richard Thomas.

Reviews

"Mr. Huston . . . can conceive a Civil War battle, and he has done so magnificently in this film. Furthermore, he has got the sense of soldiers in that long-ago day and war—their looks, their attitudes, their idioms—as suggested in the writings of the times."
—NEW YORK TIMES, OCTOBER 19, 1951

"Huston's script catches an excellent feel of timid bravado in youth that leads to foolhardy deeds, and the words he gives the characters are realistic.

The Red Badge of Courage

The use of the camera by Harold Rosson is meritorious in achieving on film the mood sought by Huston."

—VARIETY, AUGUST 15, 1951

"Despite the mutilation . . . some 70 minutes remain of John Huston's film version of Stephen Crane's Civil War classic, and much of it is breathtaking."

—PAULINE KAEL, 5001 NIGHTS AT THE MOVIES

RED MOUNTAIN

1951 • Paramount

CREDITS

Producer: Hal B. Wallis; director: William Dieterle; screenplay: John
Meredyth Lucas, George Slavin, and George W. George (based on a
story by Slavin and George); photography: Charles B. Lang Jr.
(Technicolor); music: Franz Waxman; film editor: Warren Low;
art direction: Hal Pereira and Franz Bachelin.
Running time: 84 minutes.

CAST

Alan Ladd *(Capt. Brett Sherwood)*, Lizabeth Scott *(Chris)*, Arthur
Kennedy *(Lane Waldron)*, John Ireland *(Quantrell)*, Jeff Corey *(Skee)*,
James Bell *(Dr. Terry)*, Bert Freed *(Randall)*, Walter Sande *(Benjie)*,
Neville Brand *(Dixon)*, Carleton Young *(Morgan)*, Whit Bissel *(Miles)*,
Jay Silverheels *(Little Crow)*, Francis McDonald *(Marshal Roberts)*,
Iron Eyes Cody *(Indian)*, Herbert Belles *(Indian Guard)*, Dan White
(Braden), Ralph Moody *(Meredyth)*, Crane Whitley *(Cavalry Major)*,
Dan White *(Quantrell Man)*.

(Opposite) Red Mountain: *Alan Ladd and Arthur Kennedy*

Red Mountain: *Alan Ladd, Neville Brand, John Ireland, and Arthur Kennedy* (bottom)

*J*ohn Ireland is featured as Confederate guerrilla leader William Quantrill (here spelled "Quantrell") in this Alan Ladd vehicle, with Ladd cast as a Rebel captain traveling to Colorado in an attempt to join Quantrell's band of raiders. During the course of the plot (complicated by the murder of Arthur Kennedy's character and Ladd's romantic involvement with Lizabeth Scott), Ladd eventually comes to realize that Quantrell is not the courageous Rebel fighter he pretends to be, but is, in reality, nothing more than a greedy, destructive thug, staging raids with an army of marauders not for any principle or cause but for his own glorification and enrichment.

A solid but unremarkable action film hampered by a few historical inaccuracies, *Red Mountain* was Alan Ladd's only film in which he costarred with Lizabeth Scott.

Reviews

"In accord with his usual manner, Mr. Ladd plays the whole thing with great ease, moving about and killing people with the grace of a gentleman at tea. John Ireland makes Quantrill a rascal of dark and erratic moods, while Arthur Kennedy as the renegade gold miner spends most of his time wincing painfully with a broken leg."
—NEW YORK TIMES, APRIL 26, 1952

"[Producer] Hal Wallis has tossed the full book on outdoor actioners at Red Mountain, *missing none of the standard gimmicks to keep the action boiling for the full 84-minute course."*
—VARIETY, NOVEMBER 14, 1952

The Tall Target: *Marshall Thompson, Dick Powell, and Adolphe Menjou*

THE TALL TARGET

1951 • M-G-M

CREDITS

Producer: Richard Goldstone; director: Anthony Mann; screenplay:
Art Cohn and George Worthington Yates (based on a story by Yates
and Geoffrey Homes); photography: Paul C. Vogel; film editor:
Newell P. Kimlin; art direction: Cedric Gibbons and Eddie Imazu.
Running time: 78 minutes.

CAST

Dick Powell *(John Kennedy)*, Paula Raymond *(Ginny Beaufort)*,
Adolphe Menjou *(Colonel Caleb Jeffers)*, Marshall Thompson *(Lance
Beaufort)*, Ruby Dee *(Rachel)*, Will Geer *(Homer Crowley, Conductor)*,
Richard Rober *(Lieutenant Coutler)*, Florence Bates *(Mrs. Charlotte
Alsop, Novelist)*, Leif Erickson *(Stranger)*, Peter Brocco *(Fernandina)*,
Barbara Billingsley *(Young Mother)*, Will Wright *(Thomas I. Ogden)*,
Regis Toomey *(Tim Rielly)*, Jeff Richards *(Policeman)*, Tom Powers
(Simon G. Stroud), Leslie Kimmell *(Abraham Lincoln)*, James Harrison
(Allan Pinkerton), Dan Foster *(Dapper Man)*.

*T*he
"tall target" of the title is President Abraham Lincoln, and the story deals with an assassination attempt on the newly elected president, discovered and prevented by Lincoln's bodyguard, named, ironically enough, John Kennedy.

Not directly concerned with the Civil War, *The Tall Target* is, nevertheless, an interesting film about Lincoln, since it is loosely based on a real-life incident that occurred in 1860, just before Lincoln's inauguration.

The film is small-scale but engrossing and tersely directed as Powell uncovers the would-be assassins aboard a train and thwarts their plot.

Reviews

"According to . . . The Tall Target . . . Lincoln would never have been president if it hadn't been for Dick Powell. Well, not for Mr. Powell, precisely, but for the character that he portrays in this moth-eaten melodrama about the scotching of an assassination plot. However, the yarn is so preposterous and Mr. Powell is so cussedly smug in the role of a New York detective who tips Mr. Lincoln off that illusions become somewhat scrambled. . . ."
—New York Times, September 28, 1951

"Plot was suggested by an incident in Abraham Lincoln's career which may or may not be apochryphal. Dick Powell, as a N.Y. police sergeant who briefly served as the Great Emancipator's bodyguard, discovers a plot to assassinate the newly elected president in 1861. He brings it to his superiors' attention, but resigns when rebuffed. . . . Powell is his usual forthright self in portraying the investigator."
—Variety, August 1, 1951

SPRINGFIELD RIFLE

1952 • Warner Bros.

CREDITS

Producer: Louis F. Edelman; director: André de Toth; screenplay:
Charles Marquis Warren and Frank Davis (based on a story by Sloan
Nibley); photography: Edwin Du Par (Warner Color); music: Max
Steiner; film editor: Robert L. Swanson; music direction: Murray
Cutter; art direction: John Beckman; set designer: G. W. Berntsen;
technical adviser: Ben Corbett; makeup: Gordon Bau.
Running time: 93 minutes.

CAST

Gary Cooper *(Major Lex Kearney)*, Phyllis Thaxter *(Erin Kearney)*,
David Brian *(Austin McCool)*, Paul Kelly *(Lieutenant Colonel Hudson)*,
Phillip Carey *(Captain Tennick)*, Lou Chaney Jr. *(Elm)*, James Millican
(Matthew Quint), Martin Milner *(Olie Larsen)*, Guinn "Big Boy"
Williams *(Sergeant Snow)*, Jerry O'Sullivan *(Lieutenant Evans)*, James
Brown *(Private Ferguson)*, Jack Woods *(Sims)*, Alan Hale Jr. *(Mizzell)*,
Vince Barnett *(Cook)*, Fess Parker *(Jim Randolph)*, Richard Lightner
(Lieutenant Johnson), Ewing Mitchell *(Spencer)*, Poodles Hansford
(Corporal Hamel), George Ross *(Riley)*, Eric Hoeg *(Southerner)*, Wilton
Graff *(Colonel Sharpe)*, Ned Young *(Sergeant Poole)*, William Fawcett
(Corporal Ramsey), Richard Hale *(General Henry W. Halleck)*, Ben
Corbett *(Sergeant Major)*, Guy E. Hearn *(Calhoun)*, George Eldredge
(Judge Advocate), Rory Mallinson, Ralph Sanford *(Barflies)*, Paula
Sowl *(Woman)*, Ric Roman and Jack Mower *(Guards)*, Holly Bane
(Red), Ray Bennett *(Commissioner)*, Michael Chapin *(Jamie)*.

A

tired reworking of the standard Civil War spy plot, *Springfield Rifle* stars
Gary Cooper as a Union officer expelled from the army on fabricated
charges of cowardice so that he can spy on the Confederacy. Although
flawed by a hackneyed screenplay (from a story by Sloan Nibley, a veteran of Roy Rogers scripts), *Springfield Rifle* is buoyed by the Cooper star
quality; although Cooper was getting a bit mature for action stuff by this
point, his performance here is excellent, and he is well served by a solid
supporting cast, including Lon Chaney Jr. and Fess Parker, as well as a
good Max Steiner score.

Reviews

"Three things are shown by Springfield Rifle. . . . *The first
is that counter-intelligence—or counter-espionage—was
effectively employed on the western frontier by Union forces
at the time of the Civil War. The second is that the Springfield
rifle was a weapon of phenomenal power. And the third is that
the hard-pants-cavalry western is still a considerable
movie stock in trade."*
—NEW YORK TIMES, OCTOBER 23, 1952

*"There are realistic values in the production to set up a
story of how a foresighted Union officer masterminds
a scheme to use counter-espionage to uncover the reasons*

122

Springfield Rifle: *Gary Cooper*

Springfield Rifle: *Gary Cooper*

why a Northern cavalry post is unable to supply the mounts
needed to keep the government's army on the move in
the Southern states. . . . [Director] de Toth handles
the big, brawling sequences well."
—*VARIETY*, OCTOBER 1, 1952

THE VANQUISHED

1953 • Paramount

CREDITS

Producers: William H. Pine and William C. Thomas; director:
Edward Ludwig; screenplay: Winston Miller, Frank L. Moss, and
Lewis R. Foster (based on the novel by Karl Brown); photography:
Lionel Linden (Technicolor); music: Lucien Caillet; film editor: Frank
Bracht; art direction: Hal Pereira and Earl Hedrick;
costumes: Edith Head.
Running time: 84 minutes.

CAST

John Payne *(Rock Grayson)*, Coleen Gray *(Jane Colfax)*, Jan Sterling
(Ross Slater), Lyle Bettger *(Roger Hale)*, Willard Parker *(Captain Kirby)*,
Roy Gordon *(Dr. Colfax)*, Russell Gaige *(Reverend Babcock)*, Leslie
Kimmel *(Colonel Ellansby)*, Voltaire Perkins *(Harvey Giddens)*, Sam
Flint *(Connors)*, Freeman Morse *(Randy Williams)*, Charles Evans
(General Hildebrandt), Richard Shannon *(Lieutenant Adams)*, John
Dierkes *(General Morris)*, Karen Sharpe *(Lucy Colfax)*, Ernestine
Barrier *(Mrs. Colfax)*, Ellen Corby *(Mrs. Barbour)*, Louis Jean Heydt
(Luke Taylor), with Howard Joslin, Llewellyn Johnson, John Halloran,
Harry Cody, William Beery, Sam Harris, Jack Hill, Richard Beedle,
Richard Bartell, and Brad Mora.

A

mediocre post–Civil War melodrama, *The Vanquished* stars John Payne as a Confederate soldier, formerly imprisoned by the Union, who returns home after the war only to find that his hometown is now ruled by a crooked politician (Lyle Bettger). After Payne attempts to gather evidence in order to force Bettger out of office by legal means, Bettger frames him for murder; however, Payne eventually manages to clear himself and runs Bettger out of town. *The Vanquished* was also known under the alternate titles *Rock Grayson's Women* and *The Gallant Rebel*.

Review

> *"A mild round of costumed program entertainment is spotted*
> *in this Technicolored offering from the Pine-Thomas unit at*
> *Paramount. It puts the emphasis more on talk than action,*
> *in spinning a plot concerned with the post–Civil War*
> *Reconstruction days in the South, but will get by as*
> *acceptable for either top or bottom bookings. . . . Performances*
> *are as uninspired as the scripting, but adequate to see it*
> *through to conclusion."*
> —VARIETY, MAY 13, 1953

The Vanquished: *John Payne, Lyle Bettger, and Jan Sterling*

THE BLACK DAKOTAS

1954 • Columbia

CREDITS

Producer: Wallace MacDonald; director: Ray Nazarro; screenplay:
Ray Buffum and DeVallon Scott (from a story by Buffum); photography: Ellis W. Carter (Technicolor); music: Mischa Bakaleinikoff,
film editor: Aaron Stell.
Running time: 65 minutes.

CAST

Gary Merrill *(Brock Marsh)*, Wanda Hendrix *(Ruth Lawrence)*, John
Bromfield *(Mike Daughrety)*, Noah Beery Jr. *("Gimpy" Joe Woods)*, Fay
Roope *(John Lawrence)*, Howard Wendell *(Judge Baker)*, Robert Simon
(Marshal Collins), James Griffith *(Warren)*, Richard Webb *(Frank
Gibbs)*, Peter Whitney *(Grimes)*, John War Eagle *(War Cloud)*, Jay
Silverheels *(Black Buffalo)*, George Keymas *(Spotted Deer)*, Robert
Griffin *(Boggs)*, Clayton Moore *(Stone)*, Chris Alcalde *(Burke)*, Frank
Wilcox *(Zachary Page)*.

The Black Dakotas: *Slim Pickens with revolver*

*R*unning
a spare sixty-five minutes, *The Black Dakotas* deals with President Lincoln's attempt to forge a peace pact with the Sioux Indians so that Union troops can be transferred to the South, where they are needed in the Civil War. Learning of this, Confederate strategists dispatch a spy (Gary Merrill) to disrupt the plan and also divert a Union gold shipment to the South. Eventually it is revealed that Merrill is loyal to neither the North nor the South but is instead acting in his own selfish interests.

A standard Columbia B effort, *The Black Dakotas* at least featured a good performance by Gary Merrill and fine Technicolor cinematography by Ellis W. Carter.

Review

"With a story that happily deviates from the conventional western, **The Black Dakotas** *provides the action market with better-than-average material. The . . . screenplay . . . reaches back to Civil War times when President Lincoln was attempting to smoke the peace pipe with the Sioux nation in order that Union soldiers might be freed to fight the South."*
—VARIETY, SEPTEMBER 8, 1954

The Black Dakotas: *Gary Merrill* (center)

The Raid: *Van Heflin*

THE RAID

1954 • 20th Century-Fox

CREDITS

Producers: Robert L. Jacks and Leonard Goldstein; director: Hugo
Fregonese; screenplay: Stephen Boehm (based on the story by
Francis Cockrell, from the article "Affair at St. Albans" by Herbert
Ravenal Sass); photography: Lucien Ballard (Technicolor); music:
Roy Webb; film editor: Robert Golden.
Running time: 82 minutes.

CAST

Van Heflin *(Maj. Neal Benton)*, Anne Bancroft *(Katy Bishop)*, Richard
Boone *(Captain Foster)*, Lee Marvin *(Lieutenant Keating)*, Tommy
Rettig *(Larry Bishop)*, Peter Graves *(Captain Dwyer)*, Douglas Spencer
(Reverend Lucas), Paul Cavanagh *(Colonel Tucker)*, Will Wright *(Banker
Anderson)*, James Best *(Lieutenant Robinson)*, John Dierkes *(Corporal
Deane)*, Helen Ford *(Delphine Coates)*, Harry Hines *(Mr. Danzig)*,
Simon Scott *(Captain Henderson)*, Claude Akins *(Lieutenant Ramsey)*.

The Raid: *Van Heflin and Tommy Rettig*

I_n

The Raid, Van Heflin stars as a Confederate officer who escapes from a Northern prison with his men, fleeing to Canada and regrouping in an effort to strike back at the Union from the Canadian border. Heflin's raid, with the Vermont town of Saint Albans targeted, is delayed by forty-eight hours when a Union cavalry troop arrives but is finally staged as planned; the Saint Albans bank is robbed, and the town is burned.

This above-par action film was based on a true incident occurring in 1864. An excellent actor then at the height of his abilities, Van Heflin led a capable supporting cast that included Anne Bancroft, Richard Boone, and Lee Marvin.

The Raid: *Van Heflin* (center)

Reviews

"Depiction of a little-known incident during the Civil War, The Raid stacks up as a stirring and suspenseful entry. . . . Screenplay by Sidney Boehm is based upon the raid of a small Vermont town in 1864 by a band of Confederate soldiers crossing over from Canada to give Northerners a taste of the tragic events which have beset Southern families."
—VARIETY, JUNE 2, 1954

"Well-handled [and true] story of Confederate prisoners escaping from jail in upper New England, with Bancroft and Rettig trying to snafu their marauding."
—LEONARD MALTIN, *LEONARD MALTIN'S TV MOVIES AND VIDEO GUIDE*

Five Guns West: *Dorothy Malone and John Lund*

FIVE GUNS WEST

1955 • American Releasing Corp.

CREDITS

Producer-director: Roger Corman;
screenplay: R. Wright Campbell;
photography: Floyd Crosby (Pathe Color);
film editor: Ronald Sinclair;
music direction: Buddy Bregman.
Running time: 78 minutes.

CAST

John Lund *(Govern Sturges)*, Dorothy Malone *(Shalee)*,
"Touch" Connors *(Hale Clinton)*, Bob Campbell *(John Candy)*,
Jonathan Haze *(Billy Candy)*, Paul Birch *(J. C. Haggard)*,
James Stone *(Uncle Mime)*, Jack Ingram *(Jethro)*,
Larry Thor *(Confederate Captain)*.

A

minor western reminiscent of Republic's B oaters, *Five Guns West* starred John Lund as a Confederate officer intent on gaining control of a gold shipment in order to aid the Southern cause.

Otherwise unremarkable, *Five Guns West* has some distinction as the first directorial effort of legendary low-budget exploitation director Roger Corman. Frequent Corman collaborator Floyd Crosby was responsible for the Pathe Color cinematography, and the distributor, American Releasing Corp., would soon be renamed American International Pictures.

Reviews

"Familiar names of John Lund and Dorothy Malone, plus good color lensing for [the] wide screen, make this second offering from the American Releasing Corp. acceptable fare. . . . The entertainment values aren't all they should be for the action trade, but pic should prove out for release intentions as a bill-filler. . . . Corman doesn't supply as much drive to the action as this type subject requires, so the elements of suspense and tension present in the story aren't fully realized."
—VARIETY, APRIL 20, 1955

"Fair Corman Western, which he coscripted, about a group of Rebel soldiers who hold up a Yankee stagecoach."
—LEONARD MALTIN, LEONARD MALTIN'S TV MOVIES AND VIDEO GUIDE

Five Guns West: *Dorothy Malone*

Prince of Players: *Richard Burton*

PRINCE OF PLAYERS

1955 • 20th Century-Fox

CREDITS

Producer-director: Philip Dunne; screenplay: Moss Hart (based on the book by Eleanor Ruggles); photography: Charles G. Clarke (CinemaScope, DeLuxe Color); music: Bernard Herrmann; film editor: Dorothy Spencer; art direction: Lyle Wheeler and Mark-Lee Kirk.
Running time: 102 minutes.

CAST

Richard Burton *(Edwin Booth)*, Maggie McNamara *(Mary Devlin)*, John Derek *(John Wilkes Booth)*, Raymond Massey *(Junius Brutus Booth)*, Charles Bickford *(Dave Prescott)*, Elizabeth Sellars *(Asia)*, Eva LeGallienne *(Queen)*, Christopher Cook *(Edwin Booth at Age 10)*, Dayton Lummis *(English Doctor)*, Ian Keith *(King in* Hamlet*)*, Paul Stader *(Laertes in* Hamlet*)*, Louis Alexander *(John Booth at Age 12)*, William Walker *(Old Ben)*, Jack Raine *(Theater Manager)*, Charles Cane *(Theater Assistant)*, Betty Flint *(Lady Macbeth)*, Mae Marsh *(Witch in* Macbeth*)*, Stanley Hall *(Abraham Lincoln)*, Sarah Padden *(Mrs. Abe Lincoln)*, Ruth Clifford *(English Nurse)*, Ivan Hayes *(Bernardo)*, Paul Frees *(Francisco)*, Ben Wright *(Horatio)*, Melinda Markey *(Young Lady)*, Eleanor Audley *(Mrs. Montchesington)*, Percival Vivian *(Polonius)*, George Dunn *(Doorman)*, Ruth Warren *(Nurse)*, Richard Cutting *(Doctor)*, Lane Chandler *(Colonel)*, Steve Darrell *(Major Rathbone)*, George Melford *(Stage Doorman)*, Tom Fadden *(Trenchard)*, Henry Kulky *(Bartender)*, Olan Soule *(Catesby)*.

*I*n *Prince of Players,* Richard Burton stars as the respected nineteenth-century thespian Edwin Booth, who must bear the brunt of public scorn and hatred after his brother, John Wilkes Booth (John Derek), assassinates President Lincoln. Burton's performance is excellent and features, during the course of the film, excerpts from performances of *Hamlet, Romeo and Juliet,* and *Richard III.*

The film does play fast and loose with historical facts. A stoic Edwin Booth is shown being pelted with garbage by an irate audience shortly after Lincoln's assassination, while, in reality, Edwin retired from the theater immediately after the assassination, writing a public letter of apology for his brother John's heinous actions and finally returning to the stage (after a decent interval) to public acclaim.

Stanley Hall is cast as Lincoln; an odd choice, since Raymond Massey, who had played Lincoln in RKO's *Abe Lincoln in Illinois,* is in the cast as Burton and Derek's father, Junius Brutus Booth.

Reviews

"This booming and sentimental picture of the early career of Edwin Booth, the distinguished Shakespearean actor whose own life was a detailed tragedy, is, indeed, as much an appreciation of the strolling player in a plush, romantic age as it is a warm regard for one man's valor. . . . The burst of excitement that comes with the horrible, bloody deed of Booth's wayward brother, John Wilkes, in which he assassinates President Lincoln in Ford's Theatre, yanks the picture right out of the wallow into which it has aimlessly got."
—NEW YORK TIMES, JANUARY 12, 1955

"In the part of Edwin Booth, Burton proves why Britain's Old Vic rates him so highly. He is a performer of great competence, delighting in a part tailor-made to his talents."
—VARIETY, JANUARY 5, 1955

Prince of Players: *Richard Burton and Charles Bickford*

Seven Angry Men: *Raymond Massey and Leo Gordon*

SEVEN ANGRY MEN

1955 • Allied Artists

CREDITS

Producer: Vincent M. Fennelly; director: Charles Marquis Warren;
screenplay: David B. Ullman; photography: Ellsworth Fredericks;
music: Carl Brandt; film editors: Lester A. Sansom and Richard C.
Mayer; musical director: Carl Brandt; art direction: David Milton.
Running time: 90 minutes.

CAST

Raymond Massey *(John Brown)*, Debra Paget *(Elizabeth)*, Jeffrey
Hunter *(Owen)*, Larry Pennell *(Oliver)*, Leo Gordon *(White)*, John
Smith *(Frederick)*, James Best *(Jason)*, Dennis Weaver *(John Jr.)*, Guy
Williams *(Salmon)*, Tom Irish *(Watson)*, James Anderson *(Thompson)*,
James Edwards *(Green)*, John Pickford *(Wilson)*, Smoki Whitfeld
(Newby), Jack Lomas *(Doyle)*, Robert Simon *(Colonel Washington)*,
Dabbs Greer *(Doctor)*, Ann Tyrrell *(Mrs. Brown)*,
Robert Osterloh *(Col. Robert E. Lee)*.

Seven Angry Men

*I*n

Seven Angry Men, Raymond Massey returns to the role of abolitionist John Brown, fifteen years after playing the character in the 1940 Errol Flynn vehicle *Santa Fe Trail*. The "seven angry men" of the title are Brown and his six sons, who work diligently to free the slaves.

Although the script neither canonizes nor condones Brown, it is a good deal more coherent than the narrative of *Santa Fe Trail* had been, with Massey employing his usual hammy but undeniably commanding dramatics.

Reviews

"Mr. Massey, of course, plays the principal role, not his first go at this character on the screen, since he put in a like appearance in a vintage Errol Flynn picture called Santa Fe Trail. *. . . . Partly because of Mr. Massey's steadying, low-keyed focal performance and a script by Daniel B. Ullman that doggedly adheres to simple narration, this respectable, unmajestic little entry at least suggests the personal tragedy behind the famous insurrectionist."*
—NEW YORK TIMES, APRIL 2, 1955

"This Allied Artists release dips back into history for a story about John Brown's crusade to free the slaves. It fails to qualify as worthwhile entertainment, being slow and talky."
—VARIETY, MARCH 9, 1955

Seven Angry Men: *Jeffrey Hunter and Debra Paget*

FRIENDLY PERSUASION

1956 • Allied Artists

CREDITS
Producer-director: William Wyler; screenplay: Michael Wilson
(uncredited), adapted from the novel *Friendly Persuasion* by
Jessamyn West; photography: Ellsworth Fredericks (CinemaScope,
DeLuxe Color); music: Dmitri Tiomkin; film editors: Robert Swink,
Edward A. Biery Jr., and Robert A. Belcher; art direction: Edward S.
Haworth; set designer: Joe Kish; costumes: Dorothy Jeakins and Bert
Henrikson; makeup: Emile La Vigne; music and lyrics: "Friendly
Persuasion (Thee I Love)," "Mocking Bird in a Willow Tree," "Coax
Me a Little," "Indiana Holiday," and "Marry Me, Marry Me," by
Dmitri Tiomkin and Paul Francis Webster;
technical adviser: Jessamyn West.
Running time: 137 minutes.

CAST
Gary Cooper *(Jess Birdwell)*, Dorothy McGuire *(Eliza Birdwell)*,
Marjorie Main *(Widow Hudspeth)*, Anthony Perkins *(Josh Birdwell)*,
Richard Eyer *(Little Jess)*, Phyllis Love *(Mattie Birdwell)*, Robert
Middleton *(Sam Jordan)*, Mark Richman *(Gard Jordan)*, Walter Catlett
(Professor Quigley), Richard Hale *(Elder Purdy)*, Joel Fluellen *(Enoch)*,
Theodore Newton *(Army Major)*, John Smith *(Caleb)*, Mary Carr
(Emma, Quaker Woman), Edna Skinner, Marjorie Durant, and Frances
Farwell *(Widow Hudspeth's Daughters)*, Samantha *(The Goose)*, Russell
Simpson, Charles Halton, and Everett Glass *(Elders)*, Richard
Garland *(Bushwhacker)*, James Dobson *(Rebel Soldier)*, John Compton

Friendly Persuasion: *Gary Cooper*

Friendly Persuasion: *Anthony Perkins and Dorothy McGuire*

(Rebel Lieutenant), James Seay *(Rebel Captain)*, Diane Jergens *(Young Girl Elizabeth)*, Ralph Sanford *(Businessman)*, Jean Inness *(Mrs. Purdy)*, Nelson Leigh *(Minister)*, Helen Kleeb *(Old Lady)*, William Schallert *(Young Husband)*, John Craven *(Leader)*, Frank Jenks *(Shell-Game Man)*, Frank Hagney *(Lemonade Vendor)*, Jack McClure *(Soldier)*, Charles Courtney *(Reb Courier)*, Tom Irish *(Young Rebel)*, Mary Jackson *(Country Woman)*, Joe Turkel and James Anderson *(Poor Losers)*, Harry Hines *(Barker)*, Henry Rowland *(O'Hara)*, Ivan Rasputin *(Billy Goat)*, Donald Kerr *(Manager)*, Steve Warren *(Haskell)*, Earl Hodgins *(Shooting-Gallery Operator)*, John Pickard *(Ex-Sergeant)*, Norman Leavitt *(Clem)*, Dan Kennedy *(Buster)*.

*F*riendly
Persuasion depicts the reaction of a peaceful Quaker family to the
encroaching Civil War as a young son, played by Anthony Perkins, joins
the local militia against his family's wishes as Morgan's Raiders approach
their town.

One of director William Wyler's best films, *Friendly Persuasion* offers
fine low-key performances from Perkins and Gary Cooper, as his father, as
well as Dorothy McGuire in the role of Cooper's wife.

Screenwriter Michael Wilson fell victim to the repressive politics of
the era when he was denied screen credit due to his having invoked the
fifth Amendment when testifying before the House Un-American
Activities Committee (HUAC).

Reviews

*"Inspired by a lovely group of stories by Jessamyn West and spurred
by the sympathetic talents of Gary Cooper and Dorothy McGuire,
Mr. Wyler has brought forth a picture that is loaded with sweetness
and warmth and as much cracker-barrel Americana as has
been spread on the screen in some time."*
—NEW YORK TIMES, NOVEMBER 2, 1956

*"Wyler has had the project in mind for some eight years and brought
the property over to Allied Artists from Paramount. The time and
effort he has put into it results in a top show that will mean
much to viewers."*
—VARIETY, SEPTEMBER 26, 1956

Great Day in the Morning: *Ruth Roman*

GREAT DAY IN THE MORNING

1956 • RKO

CREDITS

Producer: Edmund Grainger; director: Jacques Tourneur;
screenplay: Lesser Samuels (based on the novel by Robert Hardy
Andrews); photography: William Snyder (SuperScope, Technicolor);
music: Leith Stevens; film editor: Harry Marker; music direction:
Constantin Bakaleinikoff; art direction: Albert D'Agostino and
Jack Okey; costumes: Gwenn Wakeling.
Running time: 91 minutes.

CAST

Virginia Mayo *(Ann Merry Alaine)*, Robert Stack *(Owen Pentecost)*,
Ruth Roman *(Boston Grant)*, Alex Nicol *(Stephen Kirby)*,
Raymond Burr *(Jumbo Means)*, Leo Gordon *(Zeff Masterson)*,
Regis Toomey *(Father Murphy)*, Carlton Young *(Colonel Gibson)*,
Donald McDonald *(Gary Lawford)*, Peter Whitney *(Phil the Cannibal)*,
Dan White *(Rogers)*.

*S*eparationist
ideology and gold-rush hysteria clash in this film, detailing the pre–Civil
War scramble for gold needed to finance the Confederate war effort.

Alex Nicol is featured as a Northern secret agent squaring off against
Rebel sympathizer Robert Stack, with Virginia Mayo and Ruth Roman
added to the proceedings for romantic interest.

Director Jacques Tourneur usually managed to generate far more
excitement in his films than he does here, but *Great Day in the Morning* is
atmospheric, if uncompelling.

Reviews

"It was a great day for Dixie, that day out in Denver on the eve
of the Civil War, [when] a handful of outnumbered Southern
gentlemen outsmarted the Yankees to send $2 million in gold
by wagon train to the Confederacy. . . . The preliminaries to
that great day—all of it in SuperScope and color—are also
standard six-gun fare."
—*NEW YORK TIMES*, MAY 19, 1956

"A prelude to the War Between the States is fought out in this . . .
actioner. The entertainment that results is sufficient to fit
the not-too-demanding requirements of the general outdoor
market. . . . Exteriors have pictorial value as lensed
by William Snyder."
—*VARIETY*, MAY 16, 1956

Great Day in the Morning: *Ruth Roman* (left) *and Robert Stack* (right)

THE GREAT LOCOMOTIVE CHASE

1956 • Buena Vista

CREDITS

Producer: Lawrence Edward Watkin; director: Francis D. Lyon; screenplay: Lawrence Edward Watkin; photography: Charles Boyle (CinemaScope, Technicolor); music: Paul J. Smith; film editor: Ellsworth Hoagland; art direction: Carroll Clark; set designers: Emile Kurt and Pat Delaney; costumes: Chuck Keehne and Joseph Dimmitt; makeup: David Newell and Louis Haszillo; music and lyrics: Lawrence Edward Watkin, Paul J. Smith, and Stan Jones. Running time: 87 minutes.

CAST

Fess Parker *(James J. Andrews)*, Jeffrey Hunter *(William A. Fuller)*, Jeff York *(William Campbell)*, John Lupton *(William Pittenger)*, Eddie Firestone *(Robert Buffum)*, Kenneth Tobey *(Anthony Murphy)*, Don Megowan *(Marion A. Ross)*, Claude Jarman Jr. *(Jacob Parrott)*, Harry Carey Jr. *(William Bensinger)*, Lennie Geer *(J. A. Wilson)*, George Robotham *(William Knight)*, Stan Jones *(Wilson Brown)*, Marc Hamilton *(John Wollam)*, John Wiley *(John M. Scott)*, Slim Pickens *(Pete Bracken)*, Morgan Woodward *(Alex)*, W. S. Bearden *(Switchman)*, Harvey Hester *(Jess McIntyre)*, Douglas Bleckley *(Henry Haney)*.

(Opposite) The Great Locomotive Chase: *Fess Parker*

*I*ₙ this live-action Disney adventure, Fess Parker stars as a Union soldier who tries to destroy Confederate supply railways by taking over a Rebel train and journeying behind enemy lines with Jeffrey Hunter, who has commandeered another locomotive, in hot pursuit. At the movie's conclusion, Parker is captured, tried, and sentence to death, having nevertheless earned the respect of his captors with his heroic actions. This slickly made film, visually impressive in its original wide-screen format, was based on a true historical incident that had provided the basis for two previous silent films, *Railroad Raiders of '62* (1911) and Buster Keaton's *General* (1927). Another Disney Civil War feature, *Johnny Shiloh* (1963), starring Brian Keith, had originally been shown as a two-part episode of *The Wonderful World of Disney* TV series.

Reviews

"Walt Disney's personal affection for antique railroad trains is indulged with delightful extravagance in The Great Locomotive Chase, *the latest of his real-life color features."*
—*NEW YORK TIMES*, JUNE 27, 1956

"Walt Disney has gone back into the historical archives for this account of a Union railroad raid into the Deep South during the War Between the States. . . . Thrill high spots are in the chase action when a Confederate conductor takes after his stolen train, first on foot, then by push car and then by locomotive, in determined pursuit."
—*VARIETY*, MAY 23, 1956

The Great Locomotive Chase: *Jeffrey Hunter (at train controls)*

BAND OF ANGELS

1957 • Warner Bros.

CREDITS

Director: Raoul Walsh; screenplay: John Twist, Ivan Goff, and Ben
Roberts (based on the novel by Robert Penn Warren); photography:
Lucien Ballard (Warner Color); music: Max Steiner; film editor:
Folmar Blangsted; art direction: Franz Bachelin;
costumes: Marjorie Best.
Running time: 125 minutes.

CAST

Clark Gable *(Hamish Bond)*, Yvonne De Carlo *(Amantha Starr)*, Sidney
Poitier *(Rau-Ru)*, Efrem Zimbalist Jr. *(Ethan Sears)*, Rex Reason *(Seth
Parton)*, Patric Knowles *(Charles de Marigny)*, Torin Thatcher *(Captain
Canavan)*, Andrea King *(Miss Idell)*, Ray Teal *(Mr. Calloway)*, Russ
Evans *(Jimmee)*, Carolle Drake *(Michele)*, Raymond Bailey *(Stuart)*,
Tommie Moore *(Dollie)*, William Forrest *(Aaron Starr)*, Noreen
Corcoran *(Young Manty Starr)*, Jack Williams *(Runaway Slave)*, Zelda
Cleaver *(Sukie)*, Juanita Moore *(Budge)*, Joe Narcisse *(Shad)*, Marshall
Bradford *(General Butler)*, Charles Heard *(Helper)*, Roy Barcroft
(Gillespie, the Overseer), Curtis Hamilton *(Jacob, the Coachman)*, Riza
Royce *(Mrs. Hopewell)*, Jim Hayward *(Sheriff)*, Larry Blake *(Town
Crier)*, Guy Wilkerson *(Minister)*, with Bob Steele, Mayo Loizeau,
June-Ellen Anthony, Carla Merry, Dan White, Jean G. Harvey, Alfred
Meissner, William Fawcett, Ewing Mitchell, Morgan Shaan, Paul
McGuire, Martin Smith, Ann Doran, Milas Clark Jr., Walter Smith,
Charles Horvath, William Schallert, Carl Harbaugh, Anthony
Ghazlo, Ann Staunton, and Robyn Faire.

Band of Angels: *Clark Gable and Yvonne De Carlo*

*I*n

Band of Angels, Clark Gable, in a virtual reprise of his *Gone With the Wind* Rhett Butler portrayal, stars as a Southern plantation owner in love with one of his slaves (Yvonne De Carlo) as the Civil War breaks out. De Carlo, having previously thought herself white, had been sold to Gable on the auction block after it was revealed she was half black. Sidney Poitier, the surly black overseer of Gable's plantation, detests his master's patronizing kindness and hates De Carlo for her romantic involvement with Gable; he joins the Union army in disgust as the North invades the South. In the end, Gable, having settled his differences with Poitier, boards a ship and sails away with De Carlo, to begin a new life with her.

Although inevitably dated in its racial attitudes, *Band of Angels* at least made a commendable attempt to face the issues at hand, and the performances of the stars, under Raoul Walsh's controlled direction, were appropriately low-key and sensitive.

Reviews

"In the film that Warner Bros. has made . . . all we get is flamboyant melodrama in big, juicy, WarnerColored blobs, with nary a thoughtful reflection at any point. . . ."
—NEW YORK TIMES, JULY 11, 1957

"[The] subject of miscegenation is explored and developed in this colorful production of the Old South. . . . Clark Gable and Yvonne De Carlo . . . deliver powerful performances. . . . Miss De Carlo is beautiful as the mulatto who learns of her true

Band of Angels: *Clark Gable* (left) *and Yvonne De Carlo* (right)

*status when she returns from a Cincinnati finishing
school to attend her father's funeral."*
—VARIETY, JULY 10, 1957

*"Flat attempt to make costume epic of Robert Penn
Warren's Civil War novel."*
—LEONARD MALTIN, *LEONARD MALTIN'S TV MOVIES AND VIDEO GUIDE*

RAINTREE COUNTY

1957 • M-G-M

CREDITS

Producer: David Lewis; director: Edward Dmytryk; screenplay:
Millard Kaufman (based on the novel by Ross Lockridge Jr.); photography: Robert Surtees (Panavision, Technicolor); music: Johnny
Green; film editor: John Dunning; art direction: William A. Horning
and Urie McCleary; set designers: Edwin B. Willis and Hugh Hunt;
costumes: Walter Plunkett; special effects: Warren Newcombe; music
and lyrics: Paul Francis Webster and Johnny Green; makeup:
William Tuttle; technical adviser: Charles H. Hagedon.
Running time: 187 minutes.

CAST

Montgomery Clift *(John Wickliff Shawnessy)*, Elizabeth Taylor
(Susanna Drake), Eva Marie Saint *(Nell Gaither)*, Nigel Patrick *(Prof.
Jerusalem Webster Stiles)*, Lee Marvin *(Orville "Flash" Perkins)*, Rod
Taylor *(Garwood B. Jones)*, Agnes Moorhead *(Ellen Shawnessy)*, Walter
Abel *(T. D. Shawnessy)*, Jarma Lewis *(Barbara Drake)*, Tom Drake
(Bobby Drake), Rhys Williams *(Ezra Gray)*, Russell Collins *(Niles
Foster)*, DeForest Kelly *(Southern Officer)*, Myrna Hansen *(Lydia Gray)*,
Oliver Blake *(Jake the Bartender)*, John Eldredge *(Cousin Sam)*, Isabelle
Cooley *(Soona)*, Ruth Attaway *(Parthenia)*, Eileene Stevens *(Miss
Roman)*, Rosebud Hayes *(Bessie)*, Don Burnett *(Tom Conway)*, Michael
Dugan *(Nat Franklin)*, Ralph Vitti "Michael Dante" *(Jesse Gardner)*,

(Opposite) Raintree County: *Elizabeth Taylor*

Phil Chambers *(Starter)*, James Griffith *(Man With Gun)*, Burt Mustin
(Granpa Peters), Dorothy Granger *(Madame Gaubert)*, Owen
McGiveney *(Blind Man)*, Charles Watts *(Party Guest)*, Stacy Harris
(Union Lieutenant), Donald Losby *(Jim Shawnessy at Age 2 1/2)*,
Mickey Maga *(Jim Shawnessy at Age 4)*, Robert Foulk *(Pantomimist in
Blackface)*, Jack Daly *(Photographer)*, Bill Walker *(Old Negro Man)*,
Gardner McKay *(Bearded soldier)*, William Challee *(First Spectator)*,
Frank Kreig *(Second Spectator)*, Janet Lake *(First Girl)*, Luana Lee
(Second Girl), Judi Jordan *(Third Girl)*, Phyllis Douglas *(Fourth Girl)*,
Sue George *(Fifth Girl)*, Nesdon Booth and Robert Forrest
(Spectators).

*I*f

nothing else, *Raintree County* demonstrates the continuing popularity of
Gone With the Wind: M-G-M spent a reported $5 million to $6 million on
this epic three-hour, seven-minute production in a failed attempt to
exploit still-potent memories of the Selznick classic.

Elizabeth Taylor and Montgomery Clift starred in this lush extrava-
ganza, which, like *Gone With the Wind*, concentrated on its female protago-
nist's emotional trials more than it did on military action. A good portion
of the generous budget was expended on Taylor's costumes alone.

Director Edward Dmytryk, a long way from his Hollywood beginnings in such B pictures as *Captive Wild Woman*, propped up the muddled
script with Taylor's potent emotional fireworks, but the final result is pro-
tracted and tiring and remained so even when the film was recut by the
studio after the lukewarm box-office response, with over twenty minutes
eliminated.

Nevertheless, both *Raintree County* and its star are lovely to look at;
the crisp Technicolor photography by Robert Surtees compensates for
many of the picture's shortcomings.

Reviews

*"The word is that more than six years were spent by writers at Metro-
Goldwyn Mayer trying to get some sort of workable screenplay out of
Ross Lockridge, Jr.'s* Raintree County, *which one book reviewer described*

Raintree County: *Montgomery Clift and Elizabeth Taylor*

as 'a great, flowing, formless amoeba of a novel' and never wrote truer words. . . . Indeed, they might well have devoted another six years to the job and done themselves much better than they have done in the time already spent."
—*New York Times*, December 21, 1957

"Raintree County is one of the biggest and costliest (estimated at $5 million) productions from Metro since its release of David O. Selznick's Gone With the Wind. *Lensed via the 'Camera 65' process (65mm negative is used and reduced to 35mm for release prints), this is a study of emotional conflicts set against the Civil War turmoil, and done with pictorial sweep."*
—*Variety*, October 9, 1957

Ride a Violent Mile: *John Agar and Penny Edwards*

RIDE A VIOLENT MILE

1957 • 20th Century-Fox

CREDITS

Producer: Robert Stabler; director: Charles Marquis Warren; screenplay: Eric Norden (based on a story by Charles Marquis Warren);
photography: Brydon Baker (RegalScope); music: Raoul Kraushaar;
film editor: Fred W. Berger; music direction: Raoul Kraushaar; art
direction: James W. Sullivan.
Running time: 80 minutes.

CAST

John Agar *(Jeff)*, Penny Edwards *(Susan)*, John Pickard *(Marshal
Thorne)*, Richard Shannon *(Sam)*, Charles Gray *(Dory)*, Bing Russell
(Norman), Helen Wallace *(Mrs. Bartold)*, Richard Gilden *(Gomez)*,
Sheb Wooley *(Jonathan Long)*, Patrick O'Moore *(Bartender)*, Rush
Williams *(Edwards)*, Roberto Contreras *(Abruzo)*, Eve Novak
(Townswoman), Mary Townsend and Dorothy Schuyler *(Dance-Hall
Girls)*, with Rocky Shahan, Norman Cram, and Karl MacDonald.

R*ide*

a Violent Mile is notable for its improbable scenario featuring Penny Edwards as a female Union spy masquerading as a dance-hall girl in order to foil a Confederate plot to trade cattle for Mexican assistance in the war. John Agar costars as a stranger who rescues Edwards from Rebel agents, then becomes enmeshed in her plans when he falls in love with her. Eventually, the Confederate scheme is defeated when Agar and Edwards incite a cattle stampede.

Review

"Confused, gap-ridden story concerns Civil War espionage
in Far West, with fantastic deal to trade Southern beef for
Mexican ports. Innocent stranger John Agar, attracted to pretty
dance-hall girl Penny Edwards, finds himself defending her from
Reb agents Richard Shannon and Charles Gray after disclosure
that she's a Union agent. Sadistic U.S. marshal John
Pickard's no help, because he turns out to be the
head Reb spy. . . . Technically, picture is
adequately mounted."
—Variety, December 4, 1957

Ride a Violent Mile: *John Agar* (left)

The Proud Rebel: *Olivia de Havilland and Alan Ladd*

THE PROUD REBEL

1958 • Buena Vista

CREDITS

Producer: Samuel Goldwyn Jr.; director: Michael Curtiz; screenplay:
Joe Petracca and Lillie Hayward (based on the story "Journal of
Linett Moore" by James Edward Grant); photography: Ted McCord
(Technicolor); music: Jerome Moross; film editor: Aaron Stell; music
direction: Emil Newman; art direction: McClure Capps; set designer:
Victor Gangelin; costumes: Mary Wills.
Running time: 103 minutes.

CAST

Alan Ladd *(John Chandler)*, Olivia de Havilland *(Linnett Moore)*, Dean
Jagger *(Harry Burleigh)*, David Ladd *(David Chandler)*, Cecil Kellaway
(Dr. Enos Davis), James Westerfield *(Birm Bates, Sheep Buyer)*, Henry
Hull *(Judge Morley)*, "Harry" Dean Stanton *(Jeb Burleigh)*, Thomas
Pittman *(Tom Burleigh)*, Eli Mintz *(Gorman)*, John Carradine *(Traveling
Salesman)*, King *(Lance, the Dog)*.

The Proud Rebel, directed with care and restraint by Michael Curtiz, presented the story of an eleven-year-old boy (David Ladd) who has become a mute as a result of the trauma experienced in seeing his home destroyed and his mother killed by Union cannon fire during the Civil War. His father (Alan Ladd) travels across the country to find a cure for his son, eventually developing a warm relationship with an attractive widow (Olivia de Havilland), with the boy regaining his voice when his father is endangered and he shouts a warning to him. The two veteran stars are excellent in this film but are overshadowed somewhat by the genuinely moving performance of young David Ladd, Alan Ladd's real-life son.

Review

"Director Michael Curtiz, except for a few lapses, has derived fine performances from the principals. Alan Ladd, who is not noted for explosive portrayals, is restrained but exceptionally expressive as the father, whose anxiety and devotion prove more powerful than pride."
—*NEW YORK TIMES*, JULY 2, 1958

"While an interesting story is presented, it's the characterizations that hold forth most strongly, topped, perhaps, by the very appealing performance of David Ladd, star's eleven-year-old son who plays Ladd's boy in the pic."
—*VARIETY*, APRIL 2, 1958

The Proud Rebel: *Alan Ladd and Cecil Kellaway*

Quantrill's Raiders: *Leo Gordon and Steve Cochran*

QUANTRILL'S RAIDERS

1958 • Allied Artists

CREDITS

Producer: Ben Schwalb; director: Edward Bernds; screenplay: Polly
James; photography: William Whitley (CinemaScope, DeLuxe
Color); music: Marlin Skiles; film editor: William Austin;
art direction: David Milton.
Running time: 68 minutes.

CAST

Steve Cochran *(Capt. Alan Westcott)*, Diane Brewster *(Sue Walters)*,
Leo Gordon *(William Quantrill)*, Gale Robbins *(Kate)*, Will Wright
(Judge Wood), Kim Charney *(Joel)*, Myron Healey *(Jarrett)*, Robert
Foulk *(Hagar)*, Glenn Strange *(Todd)*, Lane Chandler *(Sheriff)*, Guy
Prescott *(Major Mathews)*, Dan M. White *(Fred Thomas)*, Thomas B.
Henry (Griggs).

*L*eo

Gordon was featured as Confederate guerrilla leader William Quantrill in this B western directed by Edward Bernds. The budget for *Quantrill's Raiders* was tight (the hundreds involved in the real-life raid on Lawrence, Kansas, are reduced to dozens here), but Gordon's sneering, villainous performance and the tightly edited action scenes make the film work.

Edward Bernds, an unpretentious, reliable craftsman who had directed B films in the Blondie and Bowery Boys series, as well as Three Stooges shorts, works briskly here, making the most of his limited resources.

Review

"A tight, showmanly piece of film-making, Quantrill's Raiders *packs plenty of movement in its comparatively short footage and is probably the best yet of films on this guerrilla leader turned out in recent years. . . . The famous Quantrill raid on Lawrence, Kansas, when more than four hundred townspeople were killed by many hundreds of the guerrilla's men, is reduced to a simple attack on the town by less than two dozen raiders, and instead of citizens meeting death here, it's Quantrill, who actually went on to further raiding. Story leading up to this, however, is well plotted and given proper motivation, with an excellent set of characters and fast direction by Edward Bernds."*
—Variety, May 7, 1958

THE HORSE SOLDIERS

1959 • United Artists

CREDITS

Producers: John Lee Mahin and Martin Rackin; director: John Ford; screenplay: John Lee Mahin and Martin Rackin (based on the novel by Harold Sinclair); photography: William Clothier (DeLuxe Color); music: David Buttolph; film editor: Jack Murray; art direction: Frank Hotaling; costumes: Frank Bretson and Ann Peck; special effects: Augie Lohman; makeup: Webb Overlander.
Running time: 119 minutes.

CAST

John Wayne *(Col. John Marlowe)*, William Holden *(Maj. Henry Kendall)*, Constance Towers *(Hannah Hunter)*, Althea Gibson *(Lukey)*, Hoot Gibson *(Brown)*, Anna Lee *(Mrs. Buford)*, Russell Simpson *(Sheriff)*, Stan Jones *(Gen. Ulysses S. Grant)*, Carleton Young *(Col. Jonathan Miles)*, Basil Ruysdael *(Boys School Commandant)*, Willis Bouchey *(Col. Phil Secord)*, Ken Curtis *(Wilkie)*, O. Z. Whitehead *("Hoppy" Hopkins)*, Judson Pratt *(Sgt. Major Kirby)*, Denver Pyle *(Jagger Jo)*, Strother Martin *(Virgil)*, Hank Worden *(Deacon)*, Walter Reed *(Union Officer)*, Jack Pennick *(Sergeant Major Mitchell)*, Frank Graham *(Union Scout)*, Chuck Hayward *(Captain Woodward)*, Charles Steel *(Newton Station Bartender)*, Stuart Holmes *(Train Passenger)*, Major Sam Harris *(Confederate Major)*, Richard Cutting *(General Sherman)*, Bing Russell *(Dunker)*, William Forrest *(Gen. Steve Hurburt)*, Fred Kennedy *(Cavalryman)*, Bill Henry *(Confederate Lieutenant)*, William Leslie *(Maj. Richard Gray)*, Ron Hagerthy *(Bugler)*, Donald Foster *(Dr. Marvin)*, Cliff Lyons *(Sergeant)*, William Wellman Jr. *(Bugler)*, Jan Stine *(Dying Man)*, with Dan Borzage.

The Horse Soldiers: *John Wayne*

Director

John Ford had previously filmed a now-classic trilogy about the U.S. Cavalry (*Fort Apache, She Wore a Yellow Ribbon,* and *Rio Grande*), but aside from Ford's segment in the episodic *How the West Was Won* (1962), *The Horse Soldiers* is the director's only film concerned with the Civil War.

In the spring of 1863, Gen. Ulysses S. Grant (Stan Jones) dispatches a contingent of cavalrymen (led by John Wayne and William Holden) to wreak havoc behind enemy lines so that Grant can invade Vicksburg and strengthen the North's position.

This story was based on Colonel Bensam Grierson's Raid on Vicksburg, an actual historical event of the war, and Ford, as fellow director John Huston had done for *The Red Badge of Courage*, studied the Civil War photographs of Matthew Brady in order to achieve an authentic visual look for his battle scenes.

The Horse Soldiers was one of Ford's best pictures and was so successful at the box office that it quickly recouped its $3,500,000 investment.

The Horse Soldiers: *John Wayne* (center)

Reviews

"The Horse Soldiers may not be precisely the Fort Sumter, or the opening gun, of Hollywood's coming celebration of the Civil War centenary. But it could be. . . . All this is made supremely graphic and exciting by the touch of Mr. Ford, and what is more, some of it has the look of history seen through the mists of the years."
—NEW YORK TIMES, JUNE 27, 1959

"Give John Ford a company of brawny men, let him train his cameras on the U.S. Cavalry and provide a script with plenty of action and he's off on the road to glory. In The Horse Soldiers, *which involves a little-known incident in the Civil War, all these elements are present, and the picture consequently adds up to a whopping big, colorful spectacle in the "grand" tradition."*
—VARIETY, JUNE 10, 1959

The Horse Soldiers: *John Wayne*

MORE CIVIL WAR FILMS
OF THE 1950s

A

Time Out of War, a twenty-three-minute 1954 short subject, managed to capture the hopelessness of war as few more expensive features have. Director and writer Denis Sanders, adapting a story by Robert W. Chambers, examines three Civil War soldiers—two Northerners and one Rebel—on sentry duty at opposite sides of a riverbank as they agree to forget political differences and observe their own private truce. As they relax, trading coffee and tobacco across the river and talking as friends, they are suddenly reminded of the war's violence when they discover the body of a dead soldier. Burying the dead man, they sadly return to the reality of war.

Love Me Tender (1954) was the film debut of pop music icon Elvis Presley. The 94-minute-long Civil War–era tale of four brothers (Presley, Richard Egan, William Campbell, and James Drury) was directed by Robert D. Webb and featured the Presley hit "Love Me Tender." Elvis played the youngest brother, who refuses to fight in the war.

The shrewd inclusion of Presley turned an otherwise routine film into one of 20th Century-Fox's biggest hits of the season, even though the popular singer looked inevitably anachronistic in the period story, and

Love Me Tender: *Elvis Presley, Debra Paget*

was outclassed by experienced dramatic talent like Egan and Robert Middleton. Wisely, emphasis was placed on Elvis's considerable singing ability, a simple formula that would later prove successful in a screen career of largely mediocre but undeniably profitable films.

Debra Paget, who appeared in Cecil B. DeMille's epic *Ten Commandments* the same year, served as Presley's decorative love interest.

The original title of *Love Me Tender* was to have been *The Reno Brothers*; it was changed postproduction.

184

THE LITTLE SHEPHERD OF KINGDOM COME

1961 • 20th Century-Fox

CREDITS

Producer: Maury Dexter; director: Andrew V. McLaglen; screenplay:
Barre Lyndon (based on the novel by John Fox Jr.); photography:
Floyd Crosby (CinemaScope, DeLuxe Color); music: Henry Vars;
film editors: Jodie Copelan and Carl Pierson; music direction: Henry
Vars; art direction: John Mansbridge; set designer: Joseph Kish;
music and lyrics: "When Love is Young" and "The Little Shepherd
of Kingdom Come" by Bob Dunham and Henry Vars
(sung by Jimmie Rodgers).
Running time: 108 minutes.

CAST

Jimmie Rodgers *(Chad)*, Luana Patten *(Melissa Turner)*, Chill Wills
(Major Buford), Linda Hutchins *(Margaret Dean)*, Robert Dix *(Caleb
Turner)*, George Kennedy *(Nathan Dillon)*, Kenny Miller *(Reuben)*,
Neil Hamilton *(General Dean)*, Shirley O'Hara *(Mrs. Turner)*, Lois
January *(Mrs. Dean)*, with John Holland, Edward Faulkner, Russ
Bender, Morris Ankrum, Nelson Leigh, Lane Chandler, Diana
Darrin, Dan Simmons, Glen Marshall, Helen Scott, Ollie O'Toole, I.
Stanford Jolley, Don Giovanni, Jerry Summers, and Glen Walters.

*T*his quiet, family-oriented story tells of an orphaned Kentucky teenager who joins the Union army during the Civil War and the difficulties he faces both during the war and readjusting to private small-town life after it ends. Based on the 1903 novel by John Fox Jr., this film was well directed by Andrew V. McLaglen, with fine performances from leads Jimmie Rodgers and Luana Patten. Academy Award–winning character actor George Kennedy made his screen debut in this film. Two previous silent-movie versions of the story had been made, in 1920 and 1928.

The Little Shepherd of Kingdom Come

The Little Shepherd of Kingdom Come

Reviews

"Bland family-type film of boy who fought for the North during Civil War and his return to rural life."
—LEONARD MALTIN, *LEONARD MALTIN'S TV MOVIES AND VIDEO GUIDE*

"Pleasant without being too maudlin."
—*MOTION PICTURE GUIDE*

Mysterious Island: *Civil War soldiers versus a giant crab*

MYSTERIOUS ISLAND

1961 • Columbia

CREDITS

Producer: Charles H. Schneer; director: Cy Endfield; screenplay:
John Prebble, Daniel Ullman, and Crane Wilbur (based on the novel
L'ile Mysterieuse by Jules Verne); photography: Wilkie Cooper and
Egil Wozholt (Eastmancolor); music: Bernard Herrmann; film editor:
Frederick Wilson; music direction: Bernard Herrmann; art direction:
Bill Andrews; special effects: Ray Harryhausen.
Running time: 100 minutes.

CAST

Michael Craig *(Capt. Cyrus Harding)*, Joan Greenwood *(Lady Mary
Fairchild)*, Michael Callan *(Herbert Brown)*, Gary Merrill *(Gideon
Spilett)*, Herbert Lom *(Captain Nemo)*, Beth Rogan *(Elena)*, Percy
Herbert *(Sergeant Pencroft)*, Dan Jackson *(Neb)*, Nigel Green *(Tom)*.

*B*ased

on fantasist Jules Verne's novel *L'isle Mysterieuse*, *Mysterious Island* follows a group of Union soldiers as they escape from a Confederate prison aboard a hot-air balloon (along with a journalist and a Rebel hostage), traveling to a remote, uncharted island in the Pacific. There they meet two beautiful women (victims of a shipwreck) and encounter the scientifically advanced Captain Nemo, marooned in an underground grotto aboard his futuristic submarine *Nautilus*.

Nemo, an antiwar activist, destroys warships with the powerful weaponry aboard his sub and seeks to eliminate the basic causes of war through the breeding of giant animals, which will theoretically eliminate hunger and poverty. The castaways encounter several of Nemo's over-sized creations before the island volcano erupts and then flee in an abandoned pirate ship, leaving Nemo behind to perish aboard the *Nautilus* in the cataclysm.

Mysterious Island benefits from eye-popping visual effects, with the giant monsters brought to life through stop-motion animation supervised by Ray Harryhausen. Most of Harryhausen's films, produced by Charles Schneer, have dealt with figures in Greek mythology; *Mysterious Island* is better than most, featuring a solid cast and an appropriately eerie music score by Bernard Herrmann. The basic story had been filmed previously, by M-G-M in 1929, by the Russians in 1941, and by Columbia as a cheap fifteen-chapter serial in 1951 and would be filmed again in 1974, but never as effectively as this 1961 Ray Harryhausen version.

Reviews

"Captain Nemo, the most engaging mad scientist who ever designed an atomic submarine to wage a war on war, is scouring the cinema seas once more. This time, the dauntless captain, in the impressive white-haired person of Herbert Lom, is resurrected just in time to save some displaced Civil Warriors from a gigantic honeycomb inhabited by tank-sized bees."
—*NEW YORK TIMES*, DECEMBER 21, 1961

Mysterious Island: *Beth Rogan and Michael Craig and the giant bee*

"The Superdynamation process and special visual effects by Ray Harryhausen have been employed by lensman Wilkie Cooper to couple incongruous, unbalanced elements on the screen with reasonable realism. Egil Wozholt's underwater photography is another asset, as is Bernard Herrmann's score. . . ."
—*VARIETY*, DECEMBER 12, 1961

191

✖

HOW THE WEST WAS WON

1962 • M-G-M

CREDITS

Producer: Bernard Smith; directors: Henry Hathaway, John Ford,
George Marshall, and (uncredited) Richard Thorpe; screenplay:
James R. Webb (based on articles in *Life* magazine); photography:
Joseph LaShelle, Charles Lang Jr., William Daniels, Milton Krasner,
and Harold Wellman (Cinerama, Technicolor); music: Alfred
Newman and Ken Darby; film editor: Harold F. Kress; art direction:
George W. Davis, William Ferrari, and Addison Hehr; set designers:
Henry Grace, Don Greenwood Jr., and Jack Mills; costumes: Walter
Plunkett; special effects: A. Arnold Gillespie and Robert R. Hoag;
music and lyrics: "How the West Was Won" by Alfred Newman and
Ken Darby; "Raise a Ruckus," "Wait for the Hoedown," and "What
Was Your Name in the States," lyrics by Johnny Mercer; "Home in
the Meadow," folk singing by Dave Guard and the Whiskehill
Singers; makeup: William Tuttle.
Running time: 165 minutes.

CAST

Spencer Tracy *(Narrator)*, Carroll Baker *(Eve Prescott)*, Lee J. Cobb
(Lou Ramsey), Henry Fonda *(Jethro Stuart)*, Carolyn Jones *(Julie
Rawlings)*, Karl Malden *(Zebulon Prescott)*, Gregory Peck *(Cleve Van
Valen)*, George Peppard *(Zeb Rawlings)*, Robert Preston *(Roger
Morgan)*, Debbie Reynolds *(Lilith Prescott)*, James Stewart *(Linus
Rawlings)*, Eli Wallach *(Charlie Gant)*, John Wayne *(Gen. William T.
Sherman)*, Richard Widmark *(Mike King)*, Brigid Bazlen *(Dora
Hawkins)*, Walter Brennan *(Colonel Hawkins)*, David Brian *(Attorney)*,
Andy Devine *(Corporal Peterson)*, Raymond Massey *(Abraham*

How the West Was Won: *Carroll Baker, George Peppard, and Claude Johnson*

Lincoln), Agnes Moorhead *(Rebecca Prescott)*, Harry Morgan *(Gen. Ulysses S. Grant)*, Thelma Ritter *(Agatha Clegg)*, Mickey Shaughnessy *(Deputy Marshall)*, Russ Tamblyn *(Reb soldier)*, Tudor Owen *(Scotsman)*, Barry Harvey and Jamie Ross *(His Sons)*, Willis Bouchey *(Surgeon)*, Kim Charney *(Sam Prescott)*, Bryan Russell *(Zeke Prescott)*, Claude Johnson *(Jeremiah Rawlings)*, Jerry Holmes *(Railroad Clerk)*, Rudolfo Acosta *(Desperado)*, Chief Weasel, Red Cloud, and Ben Black Elk *(Indians)*, Mark Allen *(Colin)*, Lee Van Cleef *(Marty)*, Charles Briggs *(Barker)*, Jay C. Flippen *(Huggins)*, Clinton Sundberg *(Hylan Seabury)*, James Griffith and Walter Burke *(Gamblers)*, Joe Sawyer *(Ship's Officer)*, John Larch *(Grimes)*, Jack Pennick *(Corporal Murphy)*, Craig Duncan *(James Marshall)*, Paul Bryar *(Auctioneer's Assistant)*, Ken Curtis *(Ben, Union Corporal)*, Walter Reed and Carleton Young *(Union Soldiers)*, Dean Stanton *(Outlaw)*, Karl Swenson *(Train Conductor)*, Jack Lambert *(Gant Henchman)*, Christopher Dark *(Poker Player)*, Gene Roth *(Riverboat Poker Player)*, Edward J. McKinley *(Auctioneer)*, Bill Henry *(Staff Officer)*, Ken Dibbs *(Blacksmith)*, Red Perkins *(Union Soldier)*, John Damler and Robert Nash *(Lawyers)*, Saul Gorss, Roy Jensen, Victor Romito, and Harvey Perry *(Henchmen)*, with Beulah Archeletta, Chuck Roberson, and Boyd "Red" Morgan.

Based

on a seven-part *Life* magazine series, this mammoth, segmented five-part epic, costing $15 million to produce in 1962 dollars, follows three generations of American pioneers from 1839 to 1889 as the western territories are civilized. Four directors—Henry Hathaway, John Ford, George Marshall, and (unbilled) Richard Thorpe—helmed the production; the third section, dealing with the Civil War, was directed by Ford and stars John Wayne as Gen. William T. Sherman, with Harry Morgan as Gen. Ulysses S. Grant. This segment dealt with an unsuccessful attempt by a troubled Confederate soldier to assassinate the two generals.

Location scenes for *How the West Was Won* were shot at Battery Rock on the Ohio River in Illinois; Courthouse Mountain in the Pinnacles National Monument, California; Chimney Rock in the Colorado Rockies; Monument Valley on the Arizona-Utah border; Paducah, Kentucky; and Custer State Park, South Dakota.

Originally exhibited at a length of 165 minutes in three-panel Cinerama, M-G-M later recut the film, and it was shown in subsequent versions running 162, 155, and (in the copyrighted version) 149 minutes.

Reviews

"How the West Was Lost *would be a more appropriate title for this dud epic, since, as conceived by the writer, James R. Webb, the pioneers seem to be dimwitted bunglers who can't do anything right."*
—PAULINE KAEL, *5001 NIGHTS AT THE MOVIES*

"It would be hard to imagine a subject which lends itself more strikingly to the wide-screen process than this yarn of the pioneers who opened the American West. . . . John Ford's directorial stint is limited to the Civil War sequences, and though that section does not contain a standout incident, there is the fullest evidence of his high professional standards."
—*VARIETY,* NOVEMBER 7, 1963

How the West Was Won: *George Peppard in the Civil War sequence following the Battle of Shiloh*

"The atmosphere of contrivance is . . . nourished by the endless parade of familiar stars, punching out stereotypes of people. Thus, the fur-trapper that James Stewart plays is not an authentic character; he's a rubber stamp of Mr. Stewart. The same is true of Gregory Peck's gambler, Debbie Reynolds's dance-hall girl, Richard Widmark's railroad builder, Thelma Ritter's cheery pioneer, John Wayne's General Sherman, Henry Fonda's buffalo hunter, and many more."
—NEW YORK TIMES, APRIL 1, 1963

Young Guns of Texas: *James Mitchum and Alana Ladd*

YOUNG GUNS OF TEXAS

1963 • 20th Century-Fox

CREDITS

Producer-director: Maury Dexter; screenplay: Henry Cross (Harry
Spalding); photography: John Nickolaus Jr. (CinemaScope, DeLuxe
Color); music: Paul Sawtell and Bert Shetler; film editors: Jodie
Copelan and Richard Einfeld; set designer: Harry Reif; costumes:
Wesley Sherrard; music and lyrics: Paul Sawtell, Bert Sheftner, and
John Herring (sung by Kenny Miller); makeup: Bob Mark.
Running time: 78 minutes.

CAST

James Mitchum *(Morgan Cox)*, Alana Ladd *(Lily Glendenning)*, Jody
McCrea *(Jeff Shelby)*, Chill Wills *(Preacher Sam Shelby)*, Gary Conway
(Tyler Duane), Barbara Mansell *(Martha Jane Canary)*, Robert Lowery
(Jesse Glendenning), Troy Melton *(Luke)*, Fred Krone *(Pike)*, Alex Sharp
(Red), Robert Hinkle *(Sheriff Hubbard)*, Will Wills *(Cowhand)*.

*T*his minor western employed the gimmick of casting the offspring of famous stars, with James Mitchum, Alana Ladd, and Jody McCrea in the leads. The thin plot involves an attempt by an expelled West Point cadet (Gary Conway) to locate his brother, who has stolen money from the Union army. Worth a look for the oddball cast, this film is otherwise tame and forgettable. Location scenes were filmed in Big Bend National Park, Texas.

Reviews

"Young Guns of Texas is a grade "B" western with some grade "A" names to adorn a marquee. Grade "A" surnames, that is. Starring . . . are James Mitchum, Alana Ladd and Jody McCrea. . . . The three co-starring youngsters needed a firm directorial hand in this vehicle. Director [Maury] Dexter didn't supply that firmness, with the result that all three seem ill-at-ease."
—VARIETY, NOVEMBER 7, 1962

"Second generation of movie stars perform satisfactorily in account of gold and girl hunt in Old West."
—LEONARD MALTIN, LEONARD MALTIN'S TV MOVIES AND VIDEO GUIDE

ADVANCE TO THE REAR

1964 • M-G-M

CREDITS

Producer: Ted Richmond; director: George Marshall; screenplay:
Samuel A. Peeples and William Bowers (based on the novel *The
Company of Cowards* by Jack Schaefer); photography: Milton Krasner
(Panavision); music: Randy Sparks; film editor: Archie Marshek; art
directors: George W. Davis and Eddie Imazu; set designers: Henry
Grace and Budd S. Friend.
Running time: 97 minutes.

CAST

Glenn Ford *(Capt. Jared Heath)*, Stella Stevens *(Martha Lou)*, Melvyn
Douglas *(Col. Claude Brackenby)*, Jim Backus *(General Willoughby)*,
Joan Blondell *(Jenny)*, Andrew Prine *(Pvt. Owen Selous)*, Jesse
Pearson *(Cpl. Silas Geary)*, Alan Hale *(Sgt. Beauregard Davis)*, James
Griffith *(Hugo Zattig)*, Whit Bissell *(Captain Queeg)*, Michael Pate
(Thin Elk), Yvonne Craig *(Ora)*, Chuck Robertson *(Monk)*, Bill Troy
(Fulton), Frank Mitchell *(Belmont)*, J. Lewis Smith *(Slasher O'Toole)*,
Preston Foster *(General Bateman)*, Harlan Warde *(Major Hayward)*,
Allen Pinson *(Private Long)*, Sugar Geise *(Mamie)*, Linda Jones *(Junie)*,
Britta Ekman *(Greta)*, Paul Langton *(Major Forsythe)*, Charles
Horvath *(Jones)*, Mary LeBow *(Mary)*, Joe Brooks *(Bannerman)*,
Richard Adams *(Courier)*, Eddie Quillan *(Smitty)*, Paul Smith and
Barnaby Hale *(Lieutenants)*, Harvey Stephens *(General Dunlap)*,
Robert Carson *(Colonel Holbert)*, Janos Prohaska *(Flagpole Sitter)*,
Clegg Hoyt and John Day *(Loafers)*, Towyna Thomas *(Law and Order
Leaguer)*, Sailor Vincent *(Deckhand)*, Bob Anderson *(Steamer Captain)*,
Gregg Palmer *(Gambler)*, Kathryn Hart and Ann Blake *(League
Ladies)*, Peter Ford *(Townsman)*, Ken Wales *(Lieutenant Aide)*.

A

trite comedy about a group of bumbling Union army misfits, *Advance to the Rear* has all the depth of an episode of the TV sitcom *F-Troop* inflated to feature-length proportions. One more in a large selection of overproduced and unfunny 1960s comedies, the film does offer an appealing performance by Stella Stevens, an underrated talent, as a supposed prostitute who is, in reality, a Confederate spy. Direction was by George Marshall, a veteran comedy specialist who helmed performers ranging from Laurel and Hardy to Jerry Lewis. *Advance to the Rear* was copyrighted under its working title, *Company of Cowards?*

(Above and opposite) Advance to the Rear: *Stella Stevens and Glenn Ford*

Reviews

"Advance to the Rear, *a broad and dinky little comedy starring Glenn Ford, Stella Stevens and Melvyn Douglas, opened yesterday. . . . If ever a picture lived up to its title, it's this one. The stars . . . flounder sheepishly in a warmed-over brew of slapstick and pratfalls as the Blues and Grays bump heads in wild confusion.*"
—NEW YORK TIMES, JUNE 11, 1964

"*Stevens as [a] Reb spy and Blondell as [a] saucy worldly woman add [the] only spice to [this] predictable slapstick comedy.*"
—LEONARD MALTIN, LEONARD MALTIN'S TV MOVIES AND VIDEO GUIDE

ARIZONA RAIDERS

1965 • Columbia

CREDITS

Producer: Grant Whytock; director: William Witney; screenplay:
Alex Gottlieb, Mary Willingham, and Willard Willingham (based on
a story by Frank Gruber and Richard Schayer); photography:
Jacques Marquette (Techniscope, Technicolor); music: Richard
LaSalle; film editor: Grant Whytock; art direction: Paul Sylos Jr.
Running time: 88 minutes.

CAST
Audie Murphy *(Clint)*, Michael Dante *(Brady)*, Ben Cooper *(Willie
Martin)*, Buster Crabbe *(Captain Andrews)*, Gloria Talbott *(Martina)*,
Roy Stricklyn *(Danny Bonner)*, George Keymas *(Montana)*, Fred
Krone *(Matt Edwards)*, Willard Willingham *(Eddie)*, Red Morgan
(Tex), Fred Graham *(Quantrill)*.

*I*t's
Confederate guerrilla leader William Quantrill (Fred Graham) versus the Arizona Raiders (led by Buster Crabbe) in this Columbia western, taking place immediately after the Civil War in Arizona Territory.

In reality, Quantrill never went to Arizona, and the Arizona Raiders weren't even formed until 1902. Such historical inaccuracies mar *Arizona Raiders*, but the film is well directed, with veteran serial hand William Witney keeping the action moving at a brisk pace.

Location scenes for *Arizona Raiders* were filmed in Phoenix, Arizona; a previous Columbia Pictures film, *The Texas Rangers* (1951), provided some source material for this production.

Review

"Name of Audie Murphy should lend potency to [box-office] chances of this fast-paced Columbia release which has [its] star . . . posing as a mem-

Arizona Raiders: *Audie Murphy and Buster Crabbe*

Arizona Raiders: *Audie Murphy* (right)

ber of a vicious gang of raiders to bring them to justice. Sound values are incorporated in the Grant Whytock production to give it polish, and there's competent acting, spirited direction and a script that keeps characters credible. . . ."
—*VARIETY*, JULY 21, 1965

Finger on the Trigger: *Rory Calhoun*

FINGER ON THE TRIGGER

1965 • Allied Artists

CREDITS

Producer-director: Sidney Pink; screenplay: Luis de los Arcos and
Sidney Pink; photography: Antonio Macasoli and Miguel Barquero
(Techniscope, Technicolor); music: José Sola; film editor: Margaritta
Ochoa; art direction: Patrick Corcoran; set designer: Edward
Bennett; costumes: Vicky; makeup: Joe Echovar;
special effects: Tony Molina.
Running time: 87 minutes.

CAST

Rory Calhoun *(Larry Winton)*, James Philbrook *(Adam Hyde)*, Todd
Martin *(Hillstrom)*, Silvia Solar *(Violet)*, Brad Talbot *(Fred)*, Leo
Anchoriz *(Ed Bannister)*, Jorge Rigaud *(Benton)*, Eric Chapman
(McKay), Benny Dues *(O'Brien)*, Axel Anderson *(McNamara)*, Tito
García *(Zubarri)*, Willie P. Elie *(Mike Daly)*, John Clarke *(Numitah)*,
Antonio Molino Rojo *(Benham)*, Juan Antonio Peral *(Tom Sharpe)*,
German Grech *(Delmer)*, Fernando Bilbao *(Mayer)*,
Sebastian Cavalier *(Slim)*.

*F*inger *on the Trigger* was a minor western starring Rory Calhoun as the leader of a Union troop journeying to Mexico immediately after the Civil War, only to discover that the local fort has been taken over by renegade Confederates. A cache of stolen gold complicates matters, and when the fort is attacked by marauding Indians, the two opposing groups of war veterans team up, melt the gold into shell casings to provide badly needed ammunition, and drive off the Indians.

Finger on the Trigger provided western regular Rory Calhoun with a good leading role, and producer-director Sidney Pink kept the action moving at a brisk pace. Although by no means an outstanding talent, Pink was responsible for a number of cheap but interesting (or at least entertaining) films in the 1960s, including the sci-fi entries *Journey to the Seventh Planet* (1961) and *Reptilicus* (1962).

Finger on the Trigger was shot on location in Spain.

Review

"BOMB [lowest rating] . . . Reb and Yankee veterans join forces to secure buried treasure while holding off hostile Indians."
—LEONARD MALTIN, *LEONARD MALTIN'S TV MOVIES AND VIDEO GUIDE*

MAJOR DUNDEE

1965 • Columbia

CREDITS
Producer: Jerry Bressler; director: Sam Peckinpah; screenplay: Harry Julian Fink, Oscar Saul, and Peckinpah (based on a story by Harry Julian Fink); photography: Sam Leavitt (Panavision, Eastmancolor); music: Daniele Amfitheatrof; film editors: William A. Lyon, Don Starling, and Howard Kunin; art direction: Al Ybarra; costumes: Tom Dawson; special effects: Augie Lohman.
Running time: 124 minutes.

CAST
Charlton Heston *(Maj. Amos Charles Dundee)*, Richard Harris *(Capt. Benjamin Tyreen)*, Jim Hutton *(Lieutenant Graham)*, James Coburn *(Samuel Potts)*, Michael Anderson Jr. *(Tim Ryan)*, Senta Berger *(Teresa Santiago)*, Mario Adorf *(Sergeant Gomez)*, Brock Peters *(Aesop)*, Warren Oates *(O. W. Hadley)*, Ben Johnson *(Sergeant Chillum)*, R. G. Armstrong *(Reverend Dhalstrom)*, L. Q. Jones *(Arthur Hadley)*, Slim Pickens *(Wiley)*, Karl Swenson *(Captain Waller)*, Michael Pate *(Sierra Charriba)*, John Davis Chandler *(Jimmy Lee Benteen)*, Dub Taylor *(Priam)*, Albert Carrier *(Capt. Jacques Tremaine)*, José Carlos Ruiz *(Riago)*, Aurora Clevell *(Melinche)*, Begonia Palacios *(Linda)*, Enrique Lucero *(Dr. Aguilar)*, Francisco Reyguera *(Old Apache)*.

*E*rratically directed by Sam Peckinpah with his customary focus on explicit violence and gore, *Major Dundee* stars Charlton Heston as a Union officer in charge of condemned Rebel prisoners. Desperately needing manpower to track down a band of renegade Apaches, Heston commutes the prisoners' sentences, and along with Union reinforcements, the motley group sets out in pursuit of Indians.

Although interesting, *Major Dundee* is flawed by a choppy, muddled narrative and is hastily assembled editorially. A completed script was not available when shooting began, and Charlton Heston later criticized the film, regretting his participation in it, as did Peckinpah.

Prior to release, the film was recut again, to 124 minutes, from the original cut's 134 minutes.

Despite the picture's drawbacks, *Major Dundee* features good supporting performances from such performers as James Coburn, Warren Oates, and Senta Berger. Jim Hutton, usually cast in bland romantic parts, makes a strong impression here.

Major Dundee was filmed entirely on location in Mexico.

Reviews

"Major Dundee *has an interesting cast, a superior visual texture, unexpected bits of character revelation and a choppy continuity that finally negates its impact. Credit the director, Sam Peckinpah, for seeking a fresh approach to the Western.*"
—*NEW YORK TIMES, APRIL 8, 1965*

Major Dundee: *Charlton Heston and Senta Berger*

Major Dundee: *Charlton Heston and Senta Berger*

"*Photography by Sam Leavitt is one of the high marks of [the]
picture, which has a rousing music score by Daniel Amfitheatrof.
Three editors are credited, including William A. Lyon, Don
Starling, and Howard Kunin, which may account in part for film's
lack of continuity through too many cutters.*"
—VARIETY, MARCH 17, 1965

"*The exploration of the ambiguities of power and honesty is subtle enough,
with the exception of a scene bearing on the racism of the Confederate men.
Embarrassingly intertwined with this, however, is a ludicrous sexual
appeal involving . . . sundry . . . luscious lovelies who seem to
have been stuck in as commercial afterthoughts.*"
—FILM COMMENT APRIL 10, 1965

SHENANDOAH

1965 • Universal

CREDITS

Producer: Robert Arthur; director: Andrew V. McLaglen; screenplay:
James Lee Barrett; photography: William H. Clothier (Technirama,
Technicolor); music: Frank Skinner; film editor: Otto Lovering;
music direction: Joseph Gershenson; art direction: Alexander
Golitzen and Alfred Sweeney; set designers: John McCarthy and
Oliver Emert; costumes: Rosemary Odell; makeup: Bud Westmore,
Frank Westmore, Rolf Miller, and Hank Edds.
Running time: 105 minutes.

CAST

James Stewart *(Charlie Anderson)*, Doug McClure *(Sam)*, Glenn
Corbett *(Jacob Anderson)*, Philip Alford *(Boy Anderson)*, Katharine
Ross *(Ann Anderson)*, Charles Robinson *(Nathan Anderson)*, James
McMullan *(John Anderson)*, Tim McIntire *(Henry Anderson)*, Paul Fix
(Dr. Tom Witherspoon), Denver Pyle *(Pastor Bjoerling)*, James Best
(Carter), George Kennedy *(Colonel Fairchild)*, Warren Oates *(Billy
Packer)*, Strother Martin *(Engineer)*, Dabbs Greer *(Abernathy)*, Harry
Carey Jr. *(Jenkins)*, Kevin Hagen *(Mule)*, Tom Simcox *(Lieutenant
Johnson)*, Berkely Harris *(Captain Richards)*, Edward Faulkner *(Union
Sergeant)*, Peter Wayne *(Confederate Corporal)*, Gregg Palmer *(Union
Guard)*, Bob Steele *(Union Guard With Beard)*, James Heneghan Jr.
(First Picket), Eugene Jackson Jr. *(Gabriel)*, Rayford Barnes *(Horace)*,
Dave Cass *(Ray)*, Hoke Howell *(Crying Prisoner)*, Kelly Thordsen
(Carroll), Lane Bradford *(Tinkham)*, Shug Fisher *(Confederate Soldier)*,
John Daheim *(Osborne)*, Joe Yrigoyen *(Marshall)*, Henry Willis, Buzz
Henry, James Carter, and Leroy Johnson *(Riders)*.

*J*ames Stewart stars as the patriarch of a Virginia farm family in 1863, steadfastly remaining aloof from the Civil War, which has spread to his area. Stewart adamantly maintains his neutral stance until his son-in-law (Doug McClure) is drafted by the South on his wedding day and another of Stewart's sons (Philip Alford) is captured by the North and accused of being a Rebel spy.

The innocent Stewart is inexorably drawn into the violence of the war as he leaves the farm in an attempt to rescue his captured son, with a third son (Patrick Wayne) and his pregnant wife (Katharine Ross) staying behind to guard the ranch, only to be murdered by looters. Eventually, Stewart has a bittersweet reunion with son Alford.

Shenandoah was actress Katharine Ross's film debut. In 1974 this story was used as the basis of a family-oriented Broadway musical of the same title.

Reviews

"This Universal release . . . is . . . too long. Under the overly detailed direction of Andrew V. McLaglen, it hits and hangs on many a static snag."
—NEW YORK TIMES, JULY 29, 1965

"Shenandoah centers, actually, upon one person, a sort of behind-the-scenes glimpse of one man's family in Virginia during the Civil War. . . . The Technicolor film . . . packs drama, excitement, and an emotional quality—particularly reflected in the climax—which should find better-than-average reception in the general market."
—VARIETY, APRIL 14, 1965

Shenandoah: *James Stewart and his on-screen family*

215

Alvarez Kelly: *Richard Widmark and William Holden*

ALVAREZ KELLY

1966• Columbia

CREDITS

Producer: Sol C. Siegel; director: Edward Dmytryk; screenplay:
Franklin Coen and Elliott Arnold (based on a story by Coen); pho-
tography: Joseph MacDonald (Panavision, Eastmancolor); music:
John Green; film editor: Harold F. Kress; music and lyrics (title song):
Johnny Mercer (sung by the Brothers Four).
Running time: 110 minutes.

CAST

William Holden *(Alvarez Kelly)*, Richard Widmark *(Col. Tom Rossiter)*,
Janice Rule *(Liz Pickering)*, Patrick O'Neal *(Maj. Albert Stedman)*,
Victoria Shaw *(Charity Warwick)*, Roger C. Carmel *(Capt. Angus
Ferguson)*, Richard Rust *(Sergeant Hatcher)*, Arthur Franz *(Captain
Towers)*, Donald Barry *(Lieutenant Farrow)*, Duke Hobbie *(John
Beaurider)*, Harry Carey Jr. *(Corporal Peterson)*, Howard Caine
(McIntyre), Mauritz Hugo *(Ely Harrison)*, G. B. Atwater *(General
Kautz)*, Robert Morgan *(Captain Williams)*, Paul Lukather *(Captain
Webster)*, Stephanie Hill *(Mary Ann)*, Indus Arthur *(Melinda)*, Clint
Ritchie *(Union Lieutenant)*.

W illiam

Holden stars as a cattleman in this offbeat Civil War–era western costarring Richard Widmark. Holden makes a deal to sell five thousand head of cattle to the Union, but he and his herd are intercepted by a villainous Confederate officer (Richard Widmark) who forces him to drive the cattle into Rebel territory.

A spectacular cattle stampede enlivens this otherwise slow-moving character study, with the normally commanding Holden oddly passive and subdued in his role, allowing a flamboyant Widmark to dominate nearly every scene they share.

Location scenes for *Alvarez Kelly* were filmed in and around Baton Rouge, Louisiana, and the film premiered in that city on October 1, 1966.

As noted here, the running time for the picture is 116 minutes, but it was also reviewed in a shorter version running 110 minutes.

Reviews

*"For this trimly entertaining Civil War drama . . . we can hail
Columbia Pictures, a cast headed by William Holden and
Richard Widmark, the director Edward Dmytryk, and a
thundering herd of twenty-five hundred steers."*
—New York Times, November 17, 1966

"Based on a true U.S. Civil War incident, Alvarez Kelly
*concerns [a] successful cattle grab engineered by Southern forces
and executed under the noses of Northern troops. Outdoor
action sequences, including an exciting stampede, enliven a tame
script. . . . William Holden and Richard Widmark are the
marquee bait for Sol C. Siegel's production. . . ."*
—Variety, October 5, 1966

Alvarez Kelly: *William Holden and Janice Rule*

The Fastest Guitar Alive: *Roy Orbison's (right) one film*

THE FASTEST GUITAR ALIVE

1967 • M-G-M

CREDITS

Producer: Sam Katzman; director: Michael Moore; screenplay:
Robert E. Kent; photography: W. Wallace Kelley (Metrocolor); music:
Fred Karger; film editor: Ben Lewis; art direction: George W. Davis
and Merrill Pye; set designers: Henry Grace and Joseph J. Stone;
music and lyrics: "Pistolero," "Good Time Party," "Whirlwind,"
"Rollin' On," "River," "Medicine Man," and "The Fastest Guitar
Alive" by Roy Orbison and Bill Dees; "Snuggle Huggle"
by Fred Karger.
Running time: 87 minutes.

CAST

Roy Orbison *(Johnny)*, Sammy Jackson *(Steve)*, Maggie Pierce *(Flo)*,
Joan Freeman *(Sue)*, Lyle Bettger *(Charlie)*, John Doucette *(Sheriff Max
Cooper)*, Patricia Donahue *(Stella)*, Ben Cooper *(Rink)*, Ben Lessy
(*(Indian Chief)*, Douglas Kennedy *(Joe)*, Len Hendry *(Deputy)*, Iron
Eyes Cody *(First Indian)*, Sam the Sham *(First Expressman)*, Wilda
Taylor *(Emily)*, Victoria Carroll *(Margie)*, Maria Korda *(Tanya)*,
Poupee Camin *(Carmen)*.

*P*opular country-and-western singer Roy Orbison was cast in this minor oater as a Confederate spy stealing a shipment of Union gold. Producer Sam Katzman was obviously trying to emulate an Elvis Presley vehicle by showcasing Orbison, but the movie failed to register with the public. Orbison, a commanding musical talent, proved to be a less-than-charismatic actor; as a result he was given no fewer than eight songs to sing while playing a trick guitar that doubled as a shotgun!

Reviews

"The Fastest Guitar Alive, which marks the film debut of Nashville-sounding Roy Orbison, is a hybrid: a Civil War comedy with songs and kooky Indians. Produced by Sam Katzman to showcase Orbison's songs, [the] pic is occasionally amusing, more often silly, but well-made trivia. . . . Director Michael Moore, recently graduated from first assistant ranks, has done a fair job within the low-budget bounds imposed."
—VARIETY, MAY 2, 1967

". . . poor action tale. . . . Worth catching only for [the] novelty of Orbison's performance."
—LEONARD MALTIN, LEONARD MALTIN'S TV MOVIES AND VIDEO GUIDE

THE GOOD, THE BAD, AND THE UGLY

1967 • United Artists

CREDITS

Producer: Alberto Grimaldi; director: Sergio Leone; screenplay:
Luciano Vincenzoni and Sergio Leone (based on a story by Age-
Scarpelli, Vincenzoni, and Leone); photography: Torino Delli Colli
(Techniscope, Technicolor); music: Ennio Moricone; film editors:
Nino Baragli and Eugenio Alabiso; music direction: Bruno Nicolai;
art direction: Carlo Simi; costumes: Carlo Simi;
special effects: Eros Bacciucchi.
Running time: 161 minutes.

CAST

Clint Eastwood *(Joe)*, Eli Wallach *(Tuco)*, Lee Van Cleef *(Setenza)*, with
Aldo Giuffre, Chelo Alonso, Mario Braga, Luigi Pistilli, Rada
Rassimov, Enzo Petito, Claudio Scarchilli, Livio Lorenson, Antonio
Casale, Sandro Sarchilli, Benito Stefanelli, Angelo Novi, Silvana
Bacci, Antonio Casas, and Aldo Sambrell.

The Good, the Bad, and the Ugly: *Clint Eastwood and Eli Wallach*

*F*ailing

to achieve any noteworthy success in Hollywood, actor Clint Eastwood traveled to Italy and earned international stardom as the taciturn lead in a series of westerns directed by Sergio Leone. *A Fistful of Dollars* (1964) and *For a Few Dollars More* (1967) had established Eastwood, the iconoclastic "Man With No Name," as a box-office commodity to be reckoned with. *The Good, the Bad, and the Ugly* (1967) was the third and best of Leone's "Dollars" trilogy.

Leone, a director of real talent who used both Eastwood's virtues and weaknesses as an actor to full advantage, constructed his films with flamboyant imagery and vigorous editing, almost single-handedly reinventing and revitalizing the tired western genre.

Explicit violence was also a key ingredient in Leone's filmic vision and is used liberally in this bold, expansive view of the American West during the Civil War, with reluctant partners Eastwood and Eli Wallach scrambling to find hidden gold before their vicious rival, Lee Van Cleef, discovers it first.

Ennio Moricone's bold, energetic music score helps enliven this film (and the other series entries). Leone's on-screen carnage—for better or worse—pushed movie violence to new heights.

Reviews

"The Burn, the Gouge, and the Mangle (*the screen name is simply inappropriate*) *must be the most expensive, pious and repellent movie in the history of its peculiar genre. . . . There is*

The Good, the Bad, and the Ugly: *Lee Van Cleef, Clint Eastwood, and Eli Wallach*

The Good, the Bad, and the Ugly: *Clint Eastwood in a nonviolent moment*

scarcely a moment's respite from the pain. Most of the scars and wounds are administered about the face, and even Eastwood, as the hero, spends a good part of the movie with his face blistered."
—*New York Times,* January 25, 1968

"The Good, the Bad and the Ugly is exactly that—a curious amalgam of the visually striking, the dramatically feeble and the offensively sadistic. Commercially, this third in the Clint Eastwood series of Italo westerns is seriously handicapped by its 161-minute running time, a length that com-plicates double-feature bookings."
—*Variety,* February 27, 1968

GUNFIGHT IN ABILENE

1967 • Universal

CREDITS

Producer: Howard Christie, director: William Hale, screenplay:
Berne Giler and John D. F. Black (based on the novel *Gun Shy* by
Clarence Upson Young); photography: Maury Gertsman
(Techniscope, Technicolor); music: Bobby Darin; film editor: Gene
Palmer; art direction: Alexander Golitzen and William D. DeCinces;
set designers: John McCarthy and John Austin; costumes: Helen
Colvig; makeup: Bud Westmore; music and lyrics: "Amy" by Bobby
Darin (sung by Bobby Darin).
Running time: 86 minutes.

CAST

Bobby Darin *(Cal Wayne)*, Emily Banks *(Amy Martin)*, Leslie Nielsen
(Grant Evers), Donnelly Rhodes *(Joe Slade)*, Don Galloway *(Ward
Kent)*, Michael Sarrazin *(Cord Decker)*, Barbara Werle *(Leann)*, Johnny
Seven *(Loop)*, William Phipps *(Frank Norton)*, William Mims *(Ed
Scovie)*, Robert Sorrells *(Nelson)*, Don Dubbins *(Scrague)*, James
McCallion *(Smokey Staub)*, Bryan O'Byrne *(Frobisher)*, Frank McGrath
(Ned Martin).

*P*op singer Bobby Darin stars as a former Confederate officer who kills a friend accidentally and, although trying his best to avoid further violence, is appointed sheriff by cattle baron Leslie Nielsen, the brother of the man Darin killed.

Although rejected by critics, *Gunfight in Abilene* is not a bad film, and Darin (who also wrote the music score) is surprisingly good in the lead. This film was a remake of an earlier 1956 film, *Showdown at Abilene,* with Jock Mahoney in Darin's role.

Reviews

"Gunfight is, generally, a rough and tough actioner with enough talent in the cast to put some meaning into William Hale's direction. Darin, as an ex-Confederate officer who is gun-shy as the result of his unintentioned killing of a friend, is offbeat casting but is quite acceptable."
—*Variety,* May 3, 1967

"Undistinguished post–Civil War account of gun-shy Darin, town sheriff, taking up arms against outlaws."
—Leonard Maltin, *Leonard Maltin's TV Movies and Video Guide*

Gunfight in Abilene: *Bobby Darin and Leslie Nielsen*

A Time for Killing: *Inger Stevens and George Hamilton*

A TIME FOR KILLING

1967 • Columbia

CREDITS

Producer: Harry Joe Brown; director: Phil Karlson; screenplay:
Halsted Welles (based on the novel *The Southern Blade* by Nelson
Wolford and Shirley Wolford); photography: Kenneth Peach
(Panavision, Pathe Color); music: Van Alexander and Mundell
Lowe; film editor: George White; music direction: Mundell Lowe; art
direction: Daniel Heller; set designer: Jack Ahern; music and lyrics:
"The Long Ride Home," by Ned Washington and Van Alexander
(sung by Eddy Arnold); makeup: Ben Lane.
Running time: 83 minutes.

CAST

Glenn Ford *(Maj. Charles Wolcott)*, George Hamilton *(Capt. Dorrit
Bentley)*, Inger Stevens *(Emily Biddle)*, Paul Petersen *(Blue Lake)*,
Timothy Carey *(Billy Cat)*, Kenneth Tobey *(Sergeant Cleehan)*, Max
Baer *(Sgt. Luther Liskell)*, Todd Armstrong *(Lieutenant Prudessing)*,
Duke Hobbie *(Lieutenant Frist)*, Dean Stanton *(Sergeant Dan Way)*,
Richard X. Slattery (Corporal Paddy Darling), Harrison J. Ford
(Lieutenant Shaffer), Kay E. Kuter *(Owelson)*, Dick MIller *(Zollicoffer)*,
Emile Meyer *(Colonel Harries)*, Marshall Reed *(Stedner)*, James
Davidson *(Little Mo)*, Charlie Briggs *(Sergeant Kettlinger)*, Craig
Curtis *(Bagnef)*, Jay Ripley *(Lovingwood)*, Dean Goodhill *(Bruce)*.

*T*his

film, depicting battles between Union and Confederate troops at the end of the Civil War, casts Glenn Ford (a Union major) and George Hamilton as officers embodying the opposing sides of the war. Director Phil Karlson dwells on the violence but manages to avoid gore, deftly building the tension and symbolic divison between Ford and Hamilton. Of note, far down in the cast, is Harrison Ford, who would later become a major box-office star in the *Star Wars* and *Indiana Jones* films as well as an Academy Award nominee for *Witness* (1985).

The working title for this film was *The Long Ride Home*. Roger Corman, the original producer-director of *A Time for Killing*, withdrew several weeks into production and was replaced by Phil Karlson. Several weeks later, film editor Monte Hellman was also replaced.

Location scenes were filmed in Zion National Park, Utah, and Glen Canyon National Recreation Area in Arizona.

Review

"Director Karlson has done some good minor
films in the past, but this isn't one of them."
—LEONARD MALTIN, *LEONARD MALTIN'S TV MOVIES AND VIDEO GUIDE*

ARIZONA BUSHWHACKERS

1968 • Paramount

CREDITS

Producer: A. C. Lyles; director: Lesley Selander; screenplay: Steve
Fisher (based on a story by Fisher and Andrew Craddock); photography: Lester Shorr (Technicolor); music: Jimmie Haskell; film editor: John F. Schreyer; art direction: Hal Pereira and Al Roelofa.
Running time: 87 minutes.

CAST

Howard Keel (*Lee Travis*), Yvonne De Carlo (*Jill Wyler*), John Ireland
(*Dan Shelby*), Marilyn Maxwell (*Molly*), Scott Brady (*Tom Rile*), Brian
Donlevy (*Major Smith*), Barton MacLane (*Sheriff Grover*), James Craig
(*Ike Clanton*), Roy Rogers Jr. (*Roy*), Reg Parton (*Curly*), Montie
Montana (*Stage Driver*), Eric Cody (*Bushwhacker*).

Arizona Bushwhackers: *Yvonne De Carlo and John Ireland*

*L*earning

of President Lincoln's request for volunteers to join the Union army and police the West, Lee Travis (Howard Keel) accepts a job as a sheriff in Arizona, running up against villainous Tom Rile (Scott Brady), who is illegally selling guns to the Indians. Western veterans John Ireland, Brian Donlevy, and Barton MacLane are also featured in this routine production, with narration by James Cagney.

Review

"[A] standard western plot undergoes a good polishing job in this latest A. C. Lyles production for Paramount . . . making it a handy actioner for its intended market. Equipped with cast names which should find ready response from oater trade, [the] film has been put together with the type of values that pay off."
—Variety, February 14, 1968

Arizona Bushwhackers: *Howard Keel and John Ireland*

Custer of the West: *Robert Shaw* (foreground)

CUSTER OF THE WEST

1968 • Cinerama

CREDITS

Producers: Philip Yordan and Louis Dolivet; executive producer:
Irving Lerner; directors: Robert Siodmak and (Civil War sequences)
Irving Lerner; screenplay: Bernard Gordon and Julian Halevy; pho-
tography: Cecilio Paniagua (Cinerama, Technicolor); music:
Bernardo Segall; film editor: Maurice Rootes; art direction: Jean
d'Eaubonne, Eugene Lourie, and Julio Molina; set designer: Antonio
Mateos; Costumes: De Zarate; music and lyrics: "Marching Song,"
"Mazwell House," and "Heroes Die" by Bernardo Segall and Will
Holt; "Follow Custer," by Segall and Robert Shaw.
Running time: 143 minutes.

CAST

Robert Shaw *(Gen. George Custer)*, Mary Ure *(Elizabeth Custer)*, Jeffrey
Hunter *(Lieutenant Benteen)*, Ty Hardin *(Maj. Marcus Reno)*, Charles
Stalnaker *(Lieutenant Howells)*, Robert Hall *(Sergeant Buckley)*,
Lawrence Tierney *(Gen. Philip Sheridan)*, Kieron Moore *(Cheyenne
Chief)*, Marc Lawrence *(Gold Miner)*, Robert Ryan *(Mulligan)*.

*I*n
Custer of the West, Robert Shaw stars as the legendary Civil War–era general who finally met his end in the bloody Indian battle at Little Big Horn.

Although Shaw does well as George Armstrong Custer, he is compromised by a muddled script unsure of how to view its subject. Is Custer a monster, pushing the Indians to both his and their destruction, or a doomed hero? The scenarists either couldn't decide or were afraid to choose, and the result is an aimless narrative, hampered even further by economical location shooting in Spain, an inadequate and unconvincing substitute for the American West.

Originally, the film was supposed to have been directed by the great Akira Kurosawa (*The Seven Samurai*) but was assigned to Robert Siodmak instead, with Irving Lerner directing the Civil War sequences.

Custer of the West is also known under the alternate title *A Grand Day for Fighting*. The working title during shooting was *Custer*. *Custer of the West* was shown in Cinerama for a few road-show engagements; some prints of the film run 120 minutes.

Reviews

"Fairly ambitious bio of [the] famed general . . . suffers from [a] script that doesn't quite know how to characterize its subject. . . ."
—LEONARD MALTIN, *LEONARD MALTIN'S TV MOVIES AND VIDEO GUIDE*

"The heart-in-mouth thrills of Cinerama lensing are meshed with the legend of Custer's last stand in this Spanish-shot western. Result is capable, audience-involving adventure on the visual level, with some tinge of disappointment

Custer of the West: *Lawrence Tierney and Robert Shaw*

*about the storyline, which doesn't rise to epic stature. . . . At
the end of the Civil War, Custer is assigned to tame the Cheyenne,
whose rights under government treaty are being
whittled away by white depredations."*
—*VARIETY*, NOVEMBER 15, 1967

Journey to Shiloh: *Jan-Michael Vincent* (left) *and James Caan* (right)

JOURNEY TO SHILOH

1968 • Universal

CREDITS

Producer: Howard Christie; director: William Hale; screenplay: Gene
L. Coon (based on a novel by Will Henry); photography: Enzo A.
Martinelli (Techniscope, Technicolor); music: David Gates; film edi-
tor: Edward W. Williams; music direction: Joseph Gershenson; art
direction: Alexander Golitzen and George Patrick; set designers:
John McCarthy and James M. Walters; costumes: Edward Armand,
Tack Takeuchi, and Leslie Hall; special effects: Roland Skeete; stunts:
Paul Baxley; makeup: Bud Westmore, Dick Blair, and Jack Freeman.
Running time: 101 minutes.

CAST

James Caan *(Buck Burnett)*, Michael Sarrazin *(Miller Nalls)*, Brenda
Scott *(Gabrielle DuPrey)*, Don Stroud *(Todo McLean)*, Paul Petersen *(J.
C. Sutton)*, Michael Burns *(Eubie Bell)*, Michael Vincent *(Little Bill
Lucket)*, Harrison Ford *(Willie Bill Bearden)*, John Doucette *(Gen.
Braxton Bragg)*, Noah Beery Jr. *(Sergeant Barnes)*, Tisha Sterling
(Airybelle Sumner), James Gammon *(Tellis Yeager)*, Brian Avery *(Carter
Claiborne)*, Clarke Gordon *(Col. Mirabeau Cooney)*, Robert Pine
(Collins), Sean Kennedy *(Custis Claiborne)*, Wesley Lau *(Colonel
Boykin)*, Chet Stratton *(Mr. Claiborne)*, Bing Russell *(Greybeard)*, Lane
Bradford *(Case Pettibone)*, Rex Ingram *(Jacob)*, Charles Lampkin
(Edward), Myron Healey *(Sheriff Briggs)*, Eileen Wesson *(Ella
Newsome)*, Albert Popwell *(Samuel)*.

241

A

group of young volunteers from Texas, led by James Caan, travel across the country to join Rebel forces before the Battle of Shiloh begins. Their fresh-faced idealism gradually turns to despair as they realize the grim reality of war and one by one meet their unfortunate end. Caan, one arm amputated as a result of battle wounds, is finally sent home to Texas by a sympathetic Confederate general who hears his story. Filmed at the height of the Vietnam War, *Journey to Shiloh* was obviously intended as an allegorical commentary on that divisive conflict.

Reviews

"Successful programmers are not simply failed "A" productions, as Universal's Journey to Shiloh *clearly demonstrates. Announced two years ago as Mervyn LeRoy's next producer-director assignment after completing* Moment to Moment, *the project was temporarily shelved after he and the studio parted company shortly thereafter. What was originally intended as a big-budget western with "serious" overtones has now emerged, under producer Howard Christie and director William Hale, as a dull, talky and half-heartedly pretentious oater."*
—VARIETY, MAY 15, 1968

An intriguing little film, this is sadly marred by extensive distributor and producer cuts. . . . Hale directs his inexperienced cast of Universal juveniles with assurance."
—THE FILM ENCYCLOPEDIA: THE WESTERN

"Limp Civil War programmer about young Texans anxious to engage in battle."
—LEONARD MALTIN, LEONARD MALTIN'S TV MOVIES AND VIDEO GUIDE

Journey to Shiloh: *Michael Sarrazin* (left)

THE DESPERADOS

1969 • Columbia

CREDITS
Producer: Irving Allen; director: Henry Levin; screenplay: Walter Brough (based on a story by Clarke Reynolds); photography: Sam Leavitt (Technicolor); music: David Whitaker; film editor: Geoffrey Foot; art direction: José Alguero; special effects: Bill Warrington. Running time: 90 minutes.

CAST
Vince Edwards *(David Galt)*, Jack Palance *(Parson Josiah Galt)*, George Maharis *(Jacob Galt)*, Neville Brand *(Sheriff Kilpatrick)*, Sylvia Syms *(Laura)*, Christian Roberts *(Adam Galt)*, Kate O'Mara *(Adah)*, Kenneth Cope *(Carlin)*, John Paul *(Lacey)*, Patrick Holt *(Haller)*, Christopher Malcolm *(Gregg)*, John Clarke *(Bandit)*, Benjamin Edney *(Pauly)*.

(Opposite) The Desperados: *Jack Palance*

245

*T*his violent western starred Jack Palance as the bloodthirsty head of a Confederate guerrilla family that continues its destructive actions even after the Civil War has ended. One of Palance's sons, Vince Edwards, rejects his family's violence and leaves for a new life in Texas, only to confront his murderous family again six years later in a vicious battle. The film is well directed but excessively violent, with Jack Palance way over the top in an eye-bulging performance as the Quantrill-like antagonist.

Reviews

"The Desperados is a hard-action post–Civil War western of the type that generally meets with favorable [box-office] reaction in its intended market. Irving Allen production . . . packs enough interest to keep audiences engaged. Star names of Vince Edwards and George Maharis, of TV fame, and Jack Palance may boost chances at turnstiles. Palance plays a Quantrill-type character who parades as a Confederate commander during closing days of Civil War."
—Variety, April 30, 1969

"Civil War deserters ravage the West. Not bad."
—Leonard Maltin, *Leonard Maltin's TV Movies and Video Guide*

"This is an indifferent Western. Palance is the Confederate fanatic of a parson whose guerilla band, which includes three of his sons, continues raping and looting after the end of the Civil War. . . . The family destroys one another in a bloody and gruesome fashion."
—The Film Encyclopedia: The Western

THE UNDEFEATED

1969 • 20th Century-Fox

CREDITS

Producer: Robert L. Jacks; director: Andrew V. McLaglen; screenplay: James Lee Barrett (based on a story by Stanley L. Hough); photography: William Clothier (Panavision, DeLuxe Color); music: Hugo Montenegro; film editor: Robert Simpson; music direction: Hugo Montenegro; art direction: Carl Anderson; set designers: Walter M. Scott and Chester L. Bayhi; costumes: Bill Thomas; special effects: L. B. Abbott and Art Cruikshank; makeup: Dan Striepke; stunts: Hal Needham.
Running time: 119 minutes.

CAST

John Wayne *(Col. John Henry Thomas)*, Rock Hudson *(Col. James Langdon)*, Tony Aguilar *(General Rojas)*, Roman Gabriel *(Blue Boy)*, Marian McCargo *(Ann Langdon)*, Lee Meriwether *(Margaret Langdon)*, Merlin Olsen *(Big George)*, Melissa Newman *(Charlotte Langdon)*, Bruce Cabot *(Jeff Newby)*, Jan-Michael Vincent *(Bubba Wilkes)*, Ben Johnson *(Short Grub)*, Edward Faulkner *(Anderson)*, Harry Carey Jr. *(Webster)*, Royal Dano *(Major Sanders)*, Richard Mulligan *(Dan Morse)*, Paul Fix *(Gen. Joe Masters)*, Carlos Rivas *(Díaz)*, John Agar *(Christian)*, Guy Raymond *(Giles)*, Don Collier *(Goodyear)*, Big John Hamilton *(Mudlow)*, Dub Taylor *(McCartney)*, Henry Beckman *(Thad Benedict)*, Victor Junco *(Major Tapia)*, Robert Donner *(Judd Mailer)*, Pedro Armendariz Jr. *(Escalante)*, James Dobson *(Jamison)*, Rudy Díaz *(Sanchez)*, Richard Angaroia *(Pétain)*, James McEachin *(Jimmy Collins)*, Gregg Palmer *(Parker)*, Juan García *(Colonel Gomez)*, Kiel Martin *(Union Runner)*, Bob Gravage *(Joe Hicks)*, Chuck Roberson *(Yankee Officer)*.

The Undefeated: *John Wayne*

Union

colonel John Wayne attempts to herd three thousand horses into Mexico, joining up with Confederate colonel Rock Hudson and his men in a battle against Mexican bandits.

A disappointingly routine western, *The Undefeated* holds little interest beyond the novelty of Wayne and Hudson costarring; the director, Andrew V. McLaglen, tries to imitate John Ford's distinctive style but fails. The film is not bad, but definitely less than what an audience would expect from Wayne, especially in comparison with a far better Wayne vehicle, *True Grit*, released the same year. The cinematography for *The Undefeated* was by frequent Ford collaborator William Clothier.

The Undefeated: *Rock Hudson*

Reviews

"Watching this ambitious, perspiring 20th Century-Fox exercise, which must have left even Wayne saddle-sore, it is impossible to forget the miracles wrought by the great Pappy Ford, with far less, amid Civil War echoes. . . . Surprisingly, this is a movie with a soft core, for all the lingering ironies of war and some churning scenes of violence."
—New York Times, February 5, 1970

"Basically wrong is the whole uneven mood of the film. Neither Wayne nor Hudson seems to know whether they are in a light comedy or a serious drama. They are, to use the word in an exact sense, simply unbelievable."
—Variety, October 1, 1969

MORE CIVIL WAR FILMS
OF THE 1960s

*I*n

The Deadly Companions (Carousel/Pathé-American, 1961), director Sam Peckinpah's first feature after a prolific career in television, Brian Keith confronts a psychotic villain (Chill Wills) who tried to scalp him during the Civil War.

La Rivière du Hibou (1961) was a French short adapted from a story by Ambrose Bierce about the execution of a Civil War soldier and his self-deluding, imagined escape from death on the gallows in the instant before the rope tightens around his neck. An Academy Award–winning short subject, this brief film was slightly reedited and adapted as an episode of the popular CBS-TV series *The Twilight Zone* under the title *An Occurrence at Owl Creek Bridge*.

The Wild Westerners (Columbia, 1962) starred James Philbrook as a U.S. marshal attempting to deliver a gold shipment to Union troops; Nancy Kovack costarred, with Oscar Rudolph directing this Sam Katzman production.

Shot in 16 mm, the semiprofessional film *Red Runs the River* (1963), produced by Bob Jones University, was a Civil War morality play critical of the war's leadership. Bob Jones Jr. headed the cast of unknowns, with Katherine Stenholm directing.

Two Thousand Maniacs (Box Office Spectaculars, 1964) was a cheap, independently produced horror film in which two vacationing couples wind up in an isolated town, to be terrorized by murderous fiends who are really *ghosts* from the Civil War. This blood-drenched oddity was directed by schlockmeister Herschell Gordon Lewis, a specialist in such exploitation drive-in fare, with Connie Mason, a *Playboy* centerfold, in the starring role. The Civil War would not merge with the horror genre again until the release of *The Killing Box,* a 1994 release in which Civil War troops battled supernatural soldiers.

In *Vengeance* (Crown International, 1964), produced by and starring William Thouriby, a former Rebel is out for revenge against the Yankee who killed his brother. Dene Hilyard directed.

Dan Duryea played the leader of Confederates stealing Northern gold in *Incident at Phantom Hill* (Universal, 1966), costarring Robert Fuller as the Union soldier trying to recover the loot from Duryea. Earl Bellamy directed, from a script by Frank Nugent and Ken Pettus.

No More Excuses (Phantasm/Rogosin-Impact, 1968), directed by and starring Robert Downey, was a muddled, surreal underground film about a Civil War soldier who gets shot in the posterior—and somehow winds up in modern-day New York!

A group of Confederate soldiers planned to rob a Union payroll in *The Scavengers* (Cresse-Frost/Republic, 1969), also known under the alternate title *The Grabbers.* John Bliss and Maria Lesse starred, with R. L. Frost directing from a script by R. W. Cresse, who also produced.

A Bullet for Sandoval: *Ernest Borgnine and George Hilton*

A BULLET FOR SANDOVAL

1970 • Universal

CREDITS

Producers: Elio Scardamaglia and Ugo Guerro; director: Julio Buchs; screenplay: Ugo Guerro, José Luis Martinez Molla, and Frederic De Urratia; photography: Francisco Sempere (Movielab Color); film editor: Daniele Alabisco; art direction: Giancarlo Bartolini Salembeni. Running time: 91 minutes.

CAST

Ernest Borgnine *(Don Pedro Sandoval)*, George Hilton *(Warner)*, Alberto De Mendozo *(Lucky Boy)*, Leo Anchoriz *(The Padre)*, Antonio Pico *(Sam)*, José Manuel Martin *(Guerico)*, Manuel De Blas *(José)*, Manuel Miranda *(Francisco)*, Gustavo Rojo *(Guadalupano)*.

*J*ulio Buchs directed this Italian-Spanish coproduction, released by Universal. British actor George Hilton stars as a Confederate deserter who flees to Mexico in order to comfort his pregnant wife, the daughter of Mexican bandit–chieftain Ernest Borgnine. Hilton discovers that his wife has died in a cholera epidemic after giving birth and must deal with pursuing Confederate soldiers and the hateful Borgnine in the course of the story.

The success of such Sergio Leone "spaghetti" westerns as *A Fistful of Dollars* resulted in the quick importation of many other foreign efforts, none as successful at the box office as Leone's films.

A Bullet for Sandoval was filmed on location in Almería, Spain. The original Italian title was *Quei Disperati Che Puzzano di Sudore e di Morte*. The Spanish title was *Los Desperados*, and that version was 100 minutes in length. The film is also known under the alternate titles *Vengeance Is Mine, Those Desperate Men Who Smell of Dirt and Death*, and (in Great Britain) *Desperate Men*.

Reviews

"Soap opera posturing and slow pacing relegate this Italo-Spanish western to a quickie programmer. . . . However, Julio Buchs's graphically interesting staging, Francisco Sempere's photography, and the story line, a sort of sagebrush vendetta, are the elements of a much better picture."
—VARIETY, JUNE 3, 1970

"Average foreign oater, with lots of action. Ex-Confederate Hilton plots revenge on Don Borgnine."
—LEONARD MALTIN, *LEONARD MALTIN'S TV MOVIES AND VIDEO GUIDE*

"Ernest Borgnine receives credit for the portrayal of Sandoval, a haughty, angry aristocrat, but the acting is so incredibly bad that it appears that this might be someone else, skillfully made up to represent Borgnine, and doing a parody of his various mannerisms, often while wearing a sombrero several sizes too large. . . ."
—SAN FRANCISCO CHRONICLE, FEBRUARY 26, 1971

KILL THEM ALL
AND COME BACK ALONE

1970 • Fida-Centauro/Fanfare

CREDITS

Producer: Edmondo Amati; director: Enzo G. Castellari; screenplay:
Tito Carpi, Enzo G. Castellari, Scardamaglia, and Joseph Romero
Hernández (based on a story by Carpi and Castellari); photography:
Alejandro Ulloa (Techniscope, Technicolor); music: Francisco De
Masi; film editors: Tatiana Morigi Casini and Maria Luisa Soriano;
art direction: Enzo Bulgarelli; set designer: Jaime Perez Cubero.
Running time: 97 minutes.

CAST

Chuck Connors *(Clyde)*, Frank Wolff *(Captain Lynch)*, Franco Citti
(Hoagy), Leo Anchoriz *(Deker)*, Ken Wood *(Kid)*, Hercules Cortés
(Bogard), Alberto Dell'Acqua *(Blade)*, with John Bartha, Furio
Meniconi, Antonio Molino, Rojo, Alfonso Rojas, and Ugo Adinolfi.

*A*nother "spaghetti" western, this Italian-Spanish coproduction stars Chuck Connors as the leader of an outlaw gang involved in stealing gold from a Union army fort. After Connors hides the loot and is captured by the Union army, a Yankee officer (Frank Wolfe)—who had instigated the heist in the first place—tortures Connors in an attempt to find the gold's hiding place.

A crudely dubbed import, director Enzo C. Castellari at least kept the film moving quickly, providing several fast-paced action scenes, and Francisco De Masi's musical score was effective.

Location scenes were filmed in Madrid and Almería, Spain.

Star Chuck Connors, who rose to fame in America on *The Rifleman* TV series, was featured in a number of Mexican and European westerns besides this one, including *Deserter* and *Pancho Villa*.

The original Italian title of *Kill Them All and Come Back Alone* was *Ammazzali Tutti e Torna Solo*. The Spanish version, released earlier in 1969 and shortened by nine minutes, was entitled *Matalos y Vuelve*. The film is also known under the alternate title *Go Kill Everybody and Come Back Alone*.

Review

"A superior variant on The Dirty Dozen *(1967) with Connors leading a successful assault on a Union fort to steal gold only to be captured. . . . The stunt work is more realistic than usual and together with the film's fast pace*
helps paper over the gaping cracks in the script."
—*THE FILM ENCYCLOPEDIA: THE WESTERN*

Kill Them All and Come Back Alone: *Chuck Connors* (left)

Macho Callahan: *David Janssen*

MACHO CALLAHAN

1970 • Felicidad/AE

CREDITS

Producers: Bernard L. Kowalski and Martin C. Schute; director:
Bernard L. Kowalski; screenplay: Clifford Newton Gould (based on
a story by Richard Carr); photography Gerald Fisher (Panavision,
Movielab Color); music: Pat Williams; film editors: Frank Mazzola,
Fabian Tordjinann, and Jerry Taylor; production design: Ted
Marshall; art direction: José Rodriguez, Granada; set designer:
Ernesto Carrasco; costumes: Barbara Rosenquest.
Running time: 99 minutes.

CAST

David Janssen *(Diego "Macho" Callahan)*, Jean Seberg *(Alexandra
Mountford)*, Lee J. Cobb *(Duffy)*, James Booth *("King Harry" Wheeler)*,
Pedro Armendariz Jr. *(Juan Fernández)*, David Carradine *(Col. David
Mountford)*, Bo Hopkins *(Yancy)*, Richard Anderson *(Senior Officer)*,
Dianne Ladd *(Girl)*, Matt Clark *(Jailer)*, Richard Evans *(Mulvey)*,
Robert Morgan *(McIntyre)*, Anne Revere *(Crystal)*, James Gammon
(Cowboy), Ron Soble *(Second Cowboy)*, Diana Iverson *(Second Girl)*,
Curt Conway *(Judge)*, Robert Dowdell *(Blind Man)*, with Cyril
Delevanti, William Bryant, Bucklind Beery, and Mike Masters.

*T*elevision
star David Janssen (*The Fugitive*) failed in an attempted crossover to the big screen largely because of inferior vehicles like this unnecessarily violent western. Janssen plays a vengeful Union soldier who escapes from prison and pursues Lee J. Cobb, the man responsible for Janssen's incarceration. Along the way, Janssen kills a one-armed Confederate thief (David Carradine) and falls in love with the thief's wife (Jean Seberg).

Coproduced and directed by Bernard L. Kowalski, *Macho Callahan* is undermined by Clifford Newton Gould's muddled script, which fails to justify the constant on-screen violence with a moral point of view.

Reviews

"It's just an incredible western which can't defend its bloody brutality by striving toward 'realism' anywhere in the plot. . . . Direction by Bernard Kowalski wanders aimlessly, except when he apparently concentrates on getting wooden portrayals from David Janssen and Jean Seberg."
—VARIETY, AUGUST 19, 1970

"Janssen [is] miscast as [a] Civil War P.O.W. escapee out to kill [the] man who got him arrested in the first place. . . . Interesting view of [the] West, but [the] dialogue is often unbelievable."
—LEONARD MALTIN, *LEONARD MALTIN'S TV MOVIES AND VIDEO GUIDE*

RIO LOBO

1970 • Malabar-Cinema Center/NG

CREDITS

Producer-director: Howard Hawks; screenplay: Leigh Brackett and
Burton Wohl (based on a story by Burton Wohl); photography:
William Clothier (Technicolor); music: Jerry Goldsmith; film editor:
John Woodcock; production design: Robert Smith; set designer:
William Keirnan; costumes: Luster Bayless and Ted Parvin; special
effects: A. D. Flowers and Clifford Wenger; makeup: Monte
Westmore, David Grayson, and Dick Cobos.
Running time: 114 minutes.

CAST

John Wayne *(Col. Cord McNally)*, Jorge Rivero *(Capt. Pierre Cordona)*,
Jennifer O'Neill *(Shasta Delaney)*, Jack Elam *(Phillips)*, Victor French
(Ketcham), Susana Dosamantes *(Maria Carmen)*, Chris Mitchum
(Tuscarora), Mike Henry *(Sheriff Tom Hendricks)*, David Huddleston
(Dr. Jones), Bill Williams *(Sheriff Pat Cronin)*, Edward Faulkner
(Lieutenant Harris), Sherry Lansing *(Amelita)*, Dean Smith *(Bitey)*,
Robert Donner *(Whiter Carter)*, Jim Davis *(Riley)*, Peter Jason
(Lieutenant Forsythe), Robert Rothwell, Chuck Courtney, and George
Plimpton *(Whitey's Henchmen)*, Bob Steele *(Deputy Sheriff)*, Boy "Red"
Morgan *(Train Engineer)*, Hank Worden *(Hank)*, Chuck Roberson
(Corporal-Guard), William Byrne *(Machinist)*, with Don "Red" Barry,
José Angel Espinosa, Anthony Sparrow Hawk, Charlie Longfoot,
Frank Kennedy, John McKee, Stanley Corson, Chuck Hayward,
Sandra Curie, Jim Preiean, Danny Sands, and Harold Cops.

*I*n this Howard Hawks western, with the action taking place immediately after the Civil War, John Wayne stars as a Union captain teaming up with two Confederate soldiers in pursuit of a stolen gold shipment.

The film is slickly produced but limply acted, with the cast simply walking through their roles. Jennifer O'Neill and Jack Elam both turn in good performances, but Wayne, having acquired the status of a national monument by this stage of his career (1970), merely coasts along on his well-established image.

Rio Lobo was the last film directed by Howard Hawks and, though no disgrace, is a disappointing end to a legendary directorial career.

Reviews

"After most recent films, good as well as bad, Howard Hawks's Rio Lobo
. . . comes almost as a reminder of what moviemaking is all about."
—NEW YORK TIMES, FEBRUARY 11, 1971

*"Rio Lobo is the sort of western that John Wayne and producer Howard
Hawks can do in their sleep. . . . A Wayne western still creates a certain
predictable conditioned response at the box office, which should give* Lobo
a modest success."
—VARIETY, DECEMBER 2, 1970

*"There's a lot of chatter and not much conviction or feeling for
the period (the Civil War and after) in this undistinguished western, made
late in the careers of Howard Hawks and John Wayne. . . . Hawks could
sometimes redeem routine material by fresh performances, but he doesn't
seem to get with it this time. The picture is lackadaisical, with tiresome
(and demeaning) jokes about Wayne's age and girth, a spoofy tone, and
sudden bursts of violence."*
—PAULINE KAEL, 5001 NIGHTS AT THE MOVIES

(Opposite) Rio Lobo: *John Wayne*

THE BEGUILED

1971 • Universal

CREDITS

Producer-director: Don Siegel; screenplay: John B. Sherry and
Grimes Grice (based on the novel by Thomas Cullinan); photogra-
phy: Bruce Surtees (Technicolor); music: Lalo Schifrin; film editor:
Carl Pingitore; costumes: Helen Colvig; makeup: Bud Westmore.
Running time: 105 minutes.

CAST

Clint Eastwood *(John McBurney)*, Geraldine Page *(Martha)*, Elizabeth
Hartman *(Edwina)*, Jo Ann Harris *(Carol)*, Darleen Carr *(Doris)*, Mae
Mercer *(Hallie)*, Pamelyn Ferdin *(Amy)*, Melody Thomas *(Abigail)*,
Peggy Drier *(Lizzie)*, Pattie Mattick *(Kanie)*.

(Opposite) The Beguiled: *Clint Eastwood*

*P*roduced

and directed by Don Siegel (*Dirty Harry*), *The Beguiled* is one of the few big-studio "art" films, with Clint Eastwood starring as a wounded Union soldier who is afforded refuge in an isolated Southern girls' school. There he romances and manipulates—and is manipulated by—the women, with the emotional treachery escalating until headmistress Geraldine Page unnecessarily amputates Eastwood's wounded leg.

Small-scale, atmospheric, and ominous, *The Beguiled* is a unique film not suited for all tastes. Inverting Eastwood's well-established screen persona, the picture did not meet audience expectations, and many filmgoers did not enjoy seeing a victimized Eastwood fall prey to his female captors, who vengefully murder him at the conclusion.

Nevertheless, *The Beguiled* is a darkly entertaining Gothic black comedy and a refreshingly "different" entry in Eastwood's filmography.

Reviews

"The Beguiled is [Don] Siegel's twenty-sixth film, as well as his most ambitious and elaborate . . . not referring to the sets, costumes and Spanish moss–hung locations . . . but to the narrative style."
—NEW YORK TIMES, APRIL 1, 1971

"Marking a distinct change of pace for both director Don Siegel and star Clint Eastwood, Universal's The Beguiled doesn't come off, and the apparent attempt to mesh Charles Addams' style with Tennesee Williams–type material cues audience laughter in all the wrong places. Period pic doesn't look strong enough to sustain class first run bookings and would probably perform best with fast playoff."
—VARIETY, MARCH 10, 1971

"The Beguiled is dedicated to the proposition that the war between men and women is more brutal and destructive than any other kind of war, least of all the quaintly remembered War Between the States."
—VILLAGE VOICE, APRIL 8, 1971

MORE CIVIL WAR FILMS OF THE 1970S

P*leasure*
Plantation (Republic Amusements, 1970) was a near-worthless low-budget production containing a surfeit of rape and murder scenes taking place on a Southern plantation during the Civil War, with these excesses strung together into a virtually incomprehensible plot. Jerry Denby directed, with William Scope, Gerald Nomes, Karil Holmes, and Kim Bishop in the leading roles.

The Lincoln Conspiracy (Sunn Classic, 1977) was a low-budget, historically unreliable "docudrama" postulating that the assassination of Abraham Lincoln (John Anderson) was actually the result of a conspiracy masterminded by Lincoln's secretary of state, Edward M. Stanton (Robert Middleton). Bradford Dillman played John Wilkes Booth in this speculative exploitation film, directed by James L. Conway.

GLORY

1989 • Tri-Star

CREDITS

Producer: Freddie Fields; director: Edward Zwick; screenplay: Kevin
Jarre (based on the books *Lay This Laurel* by Lincoln Kirstein and *One
Gallant Rush* by Peter Burchard and the letters of Robert Gould
Shaw); photography: Freddie Francis (Technicolor); film editor:
Steven Rosenblum; music: James Horner; production design:
Norman Garwood; art direction: Keith Pain and Dan Webster; set
designer: Garrett Lewis; special effects: Phil Cory; costumes:
Francine Jamison-Tanchuck; stunts: Bob Minor;
makeup: Carl Fullerton.
Running time: 122 minutes.

CAST

Matthew Broderick *(Col. Robert Gould Shaw)*, Denzel Washington
(Trip), Cary Elwes *(Cabot Forbes)*, Morgan Freeman *(John Rawlins)*,
Jihmi Kennedy *(Sharts)*, Andre Braugher *(Searles)*, John Finn
(Sergeant Mulcahy), Donovan Leitch *(Morse)*, John David Cullum
(Russell), Alan North *(Governor Andrew)*, Bob Gunton *(General
Harker)*, Cliff DeYoung *(Colonel Montgomery)*, Christian Baskous
(Pierce), RonReaco Lee *(Mute Drummer Boy)*, Jay O. Sanders *(General
Strong)*, Raymond St. Jacques *(Frederick Douglass)*, Jane Alexander
(Shaw's Mother), Richard Riehle *(Quartermaster)*, Daniel Jenkins *("A"
Company Officer)*, Michael Smith Guess and Abdul Salaam El Razzac
("A" Company Soldiers), Peter Michael Goetz *(Francis Shaw)*, Pete
Munro *(Surgeon)*, Benji Wilhoite *(Young Soldier)*, Ethan Phillips

Glory: *A Matthew Brady-type grouping*

Glory: *Matthew Broderick as Col. Robert Gould Shaw*

(Hospital Steward), Mark A. Levy (Bigoted Soldier), Randell Haynes (Paymaster), Afemo Omilami (Tall Contraband), Keith Noble (Short Contraband), Dan Biggers (Minister), Marc Gowan (Dr. Rogers), Raymond Godshall Jr. (Dr. Thorpe), Bob Minor (Contraband Soldier), Joan Riordan (White Woman), Saundra Franks (Black Woman), Mark A. Jones (Fifty-fourth Soldier), Peter Grandfirld, Mark Margolis, Paul Desmond, Tom Barrington, Michael Fowler, Kevin Jarre, and Richard Wright (Tenth Connecticut Soldiers).

*T*he Fifty-Fourth Regiment of the Massachusetts volunteer infantry, the first unit of black troops formed by the North in the Civil War, is depicted in this excellent film directed by Edward Zwick. Starring Matthew Broderick as Col. Robert Gould Shaw, the white commander of the Fifty-Fourth, *Glory* is (sadly) the first movie examining black participation in the Union war effort. Partially based on the surviving personal letters of Robert Gould Shaw, filed at Harvard, the script, Zwick's sensitive direction, and the beautifully modulated performances of the cast (particularly Broderick, Denzel Washington, and Morgan Freeman) combine to create one of the most admired Civil War dramas ever brought to the screen.

Many previous Civil War films, even the best ones like *The Birth of a Nation, The General,* and *Gone With the Wind,* have observed the conflict from a Southern perspective (*The Birth of a Nation* notoriously so), but *Glory* avoids this common point of view, generating viewer empathy for the black soldiers, with carefully realized drama that sidesteps clichés and focuses on the human qualities of the participants.

A welcome and extremely forceful counterbalance to previous cinematic insensitivities, *Glory* is well photographed, with meticulous attention to period costume and detail, by veteran cameraman Freddie Francis.

Review

"A stirring and long overdue tribute to the black soldiers who fought for the Union cause in the Civil War, Glory *has the sweep and magnificence*

Glory: *Denzel Washington restraining Morgan Freeman*

of a Tolstoy battle tale or a John Ford saga of American history. The Tri-Star release is a courageous achievement for producer Freddie Fields, director Edward Zwick, and screenwriter Kevin Jarre to have brought forth in today's marketplace."
—VARIETY, DECEMBER 13, 1989

271

Gettysburg: *Martin Sheen and Tom Berenger*

GETTYSBURG

1993 • Turner Pictures/New Line Cinema

CREDITS
Producers: Mace Neufeld and Bob Rehme; director: Ronald F.
Maxwell; screenplay: Ronald F. Maxwell (from the novel *The Killer
Angels* by Michael Shaara); photography: Kees Van Oostrum and
Eddy Van Der Enden (color); film editor: Corky Eehlers; music:
Randy Edelman; production design: Cary White; art direction: Mike
Sullivan; set designer: Barbara Haberacht;
costumes: Michael T. Boyd.
Running time: 248 minutes.

CAST
Tom Berenger *(Lt. Gen. James Longstreet),* Jeff Daniels *(Col. Joshua
Lawrence Chamberlain),* Martin Sheen *(Gen. Robert E. Lee),* Kevin
Conway *(Sgt. "Buster" Kilrain),* C. Thomas Howell *(Lt. Thomas D.
Chamberlain),* Richard Jordan *(Brig. Gen. Lewis A. Armistead),* Royce
D. Applegate *(Brig. Gen. James L. Kemper),* Maxwell Caulfield *(Col.
Strong Vincent),* Stephen Lang *(Maj. Gen. George E. Pickett),* Sam
Elliott *(Brig. Gen. John Buford),* Richard Anderson *(Gen. George Gordon
Meade),* Kieran Mulroney *(Maj. G. Moxley Sorrel),* Ted Turner *(Lt. Col.
W. T. Patton),* John Diehl *(Private Bucklin),* Patrick Gorman *(Maj. Gen.
John Bell Hood),* Cooper Huckabee *(Henry T. Harrison),* James
Lancaster *(Lt. Col. Arthur Fremantle),* Brian Mallon *(Maj. Gen. Winfield
Scott Hancock),* Andrew Prine *(Brig. Gen. Richard B. Garnett),* John
Rothman *(Maj. Gen. John F. Reynolds),* Morgan Sheppard *(Maj. Gen.
Isaac R. Trimble),* Bo Brinkman *(Maj. Walter H. Taylor),* Patrick Stuart
(Col. E. Porter Alexander), Tim Ruddy *(Maj. Charles Marshall),* Ivan
Kane *(Capt. Thomas J. Goree),* George Lazenby *(Brig. Gen. J. Johnston*

273

Pettigrew), Warren Burton *(Maj. Gen. Henry Heth)*, MacIntyre Dixon *(Maj. Gen. Jubal A. Early)*, Joseph Fuqua *(Maj. Gen. Jeb Stuart)*, Tim Scott *(Lt. Gen. Richard S. Ewell)*, Alex Harvey *(Major Hawkins)*, Charles Lester Kinsolving *(Brig. Gen. William Barksdale)*, Ted Kozlosky *(Confederate Lieutenant)*, Henry Atterbury *(Lee's Aide)*, Graham Winton *(Maj. Gen. Robert E. Rodes)*, Curtiss Bradford *(Another Officer)*, Daniel Chamblin *(Confederate Officer)*, Patrick Falci *(Lt. Gen. Ambrose Powell Hill)*, Greg Ginther *(Rodes's Courier)*, George Heffner *(Another Officer)*, Tom Landon *(Second Texas Soldier)*, Michael Tennessee Lee *(Rebel Prisoner)*, Rick Leisenring *(Confederate Voice)*, Steve Leone *(An Officer)*, Tom Mays *(Early's Courier)*, Donal Logue *(Capt. Ellis Spear)*, Ken Burns *(Hancock's Aide)*, Frank McGurgan *(Old Sergeant)*, Peter Miller *(Pender's Courier)*, Arnold Nisley *(Sergeant)*, Ted Rebich *(Dr. Cullen)*, Curtis Utz *(First Texas Soldier)*, C. George Werner *(Another Officer)*, Joe Ayer and Eric Ayer *(Banjo and Guitar Players)*, Josh Mauer *(Col. James C. Rice)*, William Campbell *(Lieutenant Pitzer)*, David Carpenter *(Col. Thomas C. Devin)*, Dwier Brown *(Captain Brewer)*, Herb Mitchell *(Sgt. Andrew J. Tozier)*, Emile O. Schmidt *(Brig. Gen. John Gibbon)*, Daniel Baumann *(Second Private)*. There are cameo bits by Nick Nolte, Charlie Sheen, and the Gulf War hero Gen. Norman Schwarzkopf.)

*T*he 1863 battle in Gettysburg, Pennsylvania, serves as the basis for this film, produced on a large scale by cable-TV mogul Ted Turner, who appears on-screen in a small role. Apparently intended as a modern equivalent of *Gone With the Wind, Gettysburg,* although well acted by its large cast, is too crowded with characters based on historical figures for any one of them to stand out in relief and create an impression. Despite this lack of dramatic focus, *Gettysburg* does succeed as historical spectacle, capturing the chaos and horror of a monumental battle in which more than fifty thousand men died in only three days.

If there is a structural problem with *Gettysburg,* it lies in scriptwriter-director Ronald F. Maxwell's desire to avoid offending any segment of the audience by refusing to "take sides." At one point, Gen. Robert E. Lee, played by Martin Sheen, actually says, "Does it matter at all who wins?" It mattered a great deal to those involved in the actual conflict, which is why the Civil War occurred in the first place.

Many of the authentic props and uniforms used in *Gettysburg* were

Gettysburg: *Hand-to-hand combat at Little Round Top*

supplied by Civil War collectors and hobbyists who appear on-screen as battle extras, and documentarian Ken Burns—himself responsible for an excellent TV history of the war—appears in a bit part.

Reviews

"Ted Turner doesn't do anything in a small way. The premiere entry for his new feature production unit is a 4 1/4-hour epic on the biggest battle of the Civil War, and it will prove a hit with history buffs. Regular filmgoers should be captivated, too. . . . Gettysburg *succeeds as a motion pictureuu5 event and as a re-creation of a pivotal chapter of American history. After a summer of flash and sizzle, audiences may be ready for a healthy dose of substance."*
—Variety, October 4, 1993

"Magnificent, awe-inspiring re-creation of the Civil War's most famous battle. Ted Turner's answer to Gone With the Wind *serves up generous portions of emotional human drama and roaring action."*
—Leonard Maltin, *Leonard Maltin's TV Movies and Video Guide*

Sommersby: *Jodie Foster and Richard Gere*

SOMMERSBY

1993 • Warner Bros.

CREDITS

Producers: Arnon Milchan and Steve Reuther; director: Jon Amiel; screenplay: Nicholas Meyer and Sarah Kernochan (from a story by Nicholas Meyer and Anthony Shaffer, based on the screenplay *Le Retour de Martin Guerre* by Daniel Vigne and Jean-Claude Carriere); photography: Philippe Rousselot (color); film editor: Peter Boyle; music: Danny Elfman; production design: Bruno Rubeo; art direction: P. Michael Johnston; set designers: Michael Seirton and Marco Rubero; costumes: Marilyn Vance-Straker; choreography: Colleen Kelly.
Running time: 112 minutes.

CAST

Richard Gere *(Jack)*, Jodie Foster *(Laurel)*, Lanny Flaherty *(Buck)*, Wendell Wellman *(Travis)*, Bill Pullman *(Orin)*, Brett Kelley *(Little Rob)*, William Windom *(Reverend Powell)*, Clarice Taylor *(Esther)*, James Earl Jones *(Judge Issacs)*, Frankie Faison *(Joseph)*, R. Lee Ermey *(Dick Mead)*, Richard Hamilton *(Doc Evans)*, Ray McKinnon *(Lawyer Webb)*, Maury Chaykin *(Lawyer Dawson)*, Karen Kirschenbauer *(Mrs. Evans)*, Carter McNeese *(Storekeeper Wilson)*, Dean Whitworth *(Tom Clemmons)*, Stan Kelly *(John Green)*, Stephanie Weaver *(Mrs. Bundy)*.

*S*ommersby

is a remake of *The Return of Martin Guerre*, a successful 1982 French film about a man who returns home after an absence of several years, only to find that his wife and family think that he may be an impostor because he has changed so dramatically—and for the better—over the interim. *Sommersby* updates the original story from sixteenth-century France to the American Civil War, with transformed veteran Richard Gere returning home to wife Jodie Foster.

Director Jon Amiel, working from an excellent screenplay adaptation of the French original by Nicholas Meyer, Sarah Kernochan, and Anthony Schaffer, draws excellent performances from Gere and Foster, providing enough style to lift the film above the ordinary.

Sommersby was photographed in Virginia, with Richard Gere as executive producer.

Reviews

"Sommersby is an unabashedly romantic and at the same time morally intricate Civil War–era tale splendidly acted by Richard Gere and Jodie Foster. It's one of those rare occasions that the Americanization of a foreign property (here Daniel Vigne's Return of Martin Guerre*) works as well as the original. Female audiences should flock to see the Richard Gere/Jodie Foster pairing and Warners appears to have a [box-office] winner.... Nicholas Meyer and Sarah Kernochan's screenplay (from Meyer and Anthony Shaffer's story) is cogent and elegantly literate.... Helmer Jon Amiel ... is up to the challenge of the material, making it work both comme rcially and artistically...."*
—Variety, February 1, 1993

"This is the kind of film that takes you to another time and place, but despite strong performances, the characters remain aloof—and so does their plight."
—Leonard Maltin, *Leonard Maltin's TV Movies and Video Guide*

Sommersby: *Jodie Foster and Richard Gere*

279

APPENDIX:
CIVIL WAR FILMS
OF THE SILENT ERA (1903–29)

Uncle Tom's Cabin (Edison, 1903); director: Edwin S. Porter

Uncle Tom's Cabin (Lubin, 1903)

The Guerilla (Biograph, 1908); director: D. W. Griffith

In the Shenandoah Valley (Selig, 1908)

The Reprieve (Vitagraph, 1908)

Sheridan's Ride (Vitagraph, 1908)

Brother Against Brother (Selig, 1909)

The Girl Spy (Kalem, 1909); director: Sidney Olcott

In Old Kentucky (Biograph, 1909); director: D. W. Griffith

The Old Soldier's Story (Kalem, 1909)

The Rally 'Round the Flag (Kalem, 1909)

Stirring Days in Old Virginia (Selig, 1909)

Abraham Lincoln's Clemency (Pathe, 1910)

All's Fair in Love and War (Independent, 1910)

The Bravest Girl in the World (Kalem, 1910)

The Common Enemy (1910)

The Confederate Spy (1910)

The Dividing Line (Imp, 1910)

A Dixie Mother (Vitagraph, 1910)

The Flag of His Country (Thanhouser, 1910)

The Fugitive (Biograph, 1910); director: D. W. Griffith

Further Adventures of the Girl Spy (Kalem, 1910)

The Girl Spy Before Vicksburg (Kalem, 1910)

The Honor of His Family (Biograph, 1910); director: D. W. Griffith

The House with Closed Shutters (Biograph, 1910); director: D. W. Griffith

In the Border States, or A Little Heroine of the Civil War (Biograph, 1910); director: D. W. Griffith

Ransomed, or A Prisoner of War (Vitagraph, 1910)

Uncle Tom's Cabin (Thanhouser, 1910)

Uncle Tom's Cabin (Vitagraph, 1910)

The War and the Widow (Champion, 1910)

A Wartime Mother's Sacrifice (Broncho, 1910)

The Battle (Biograph, 1911); director: D. W. Griffith

The Battle Hymn of the Republic (Vitagraph, 1911); director: Lawrence Trimble

General Meade's Fighting Days (Champion, 1911)

Grant and Lincoln (Champion, 1911)

He Fought for the U.S.A. (Essanay, 1911)

Hearts and Flags (Edison, 1911)

His Trust (Biograph, 1911); director: D. W. Griffith

His Trust Fulfilled (Biograph, 1911); director: D. W. Griffith

Lieutenant Grey of the Confederacy (Selig, 1911); director: Francis Boggs

The Little Soldier of '64 (Kalem, 1911)

The Little Spy (Vitagraph, 1911)

The Lost Dispatch (1911)

One Flag at Last (Vitagraph, 1911)

Railroad Raiders of '62 (Kalem, 1911)

The Redemption of a Coward (Champion, 1911)

The Rival Brothers' Patriotism (Pathe, 1911)

The Romance of Dixie Belle (Kalem, 1911)

A Romance of the '60s (Lubin, 1911)

A Southern Boy of '61 (Kalem, 1911)

A Southern Soldier's Sacrifice (Vitagraph, 1911)

Swords and Hearts (Biograph, 1911); director: D. W. Griffith

To the Aid of Stonewall Jackson (Kalem, 1911)

Under Johnston and Lee (Champion, 1911)

The Wages of War (Vitagraph, 1911)

A Wartime Escape (Kalem, 1911)

With Sherman at Murfreesboro (Champion, 1911)

With Stonewall Jackson (Champion, 1911)

The Battle of Pottsburg Ridge (Kalem, 1912)

Blood Will Tell (Kay-Bee, 1912)

The Bugler of Battery B (Kalem, 1912)

The Cause (Kay-Bee, 1912)

The Darling of the C.S.A. (Kalem, 1912)

The Defender of the Name (Rex, 1912)

The Drummer Girl of Vicksburg (Kalem, 1912)

The Drummer of the 8th (Ince, 1912)

The Equine Spy (Solax, 1912)

The Informer (Biograph, 1912); director: D. W. Griffith

Lincoln's Gettysburg Address (Vitagraph, 1912)

The Little Turncoat (Ince, 1912)

A Man's Duty (Reliance, 1912)

None Can Do More (1912)

On Secret Service (Ince, 1912)

On the Firing Line (Bison, 1912)

The Seventh Son (Vitagraph, 1912)

Sheridan's Ride (Bison, 1912). Note: later cut by ten minutes and rereleased as After the Battle by Universal Pictures.

The Soldier Brothers of Susanna (Kalem, 1912)

A Spartan Mother (Kalem, 1912)

A True Believer (Ince, 1912)

With Longstreet at Seven Pines (Champion, 1912)

Banty Tim (1913)

The Battle of Bull Run (Bison, 1913)

The Battle of Gettysburg (Mutual, 1913), 5 reels; director: Thomas H. Ince

The Battle of Shiloh (Lubin, 1913), 4 reels; director: Joseph Smiley

Belle Boyd, a Confederate Spy (Selig, 1913)

A Black Conspiracy (1913)

The Boomerang (Broncho, 1913)

Bread Cast Upon the Waters (1913)

The Call to Arms (1913); director: Allan Dwan

The Carpenter, or The Stranger in Gray (Vitagraph, 1913)

A Child of War (Broncho, 1913)

The Colonel's Son (Kalem, 1913)

The Coward's Atonement (Bison, 1913)

The Crimson Stain (Kay-Bee, 1913)

A Daughter of the Confederacy (Kalem, 1913)

Domino's Devotion (1913)

The Favorite Son (1913)

The Fire-fighting Zouaves (Kalem, 1913)

For the Cause (ca. 1913)

The Girl of the Sunny South (American Kineto Corp., 1913), 4 reels

The Gray Sentinel (Broncho, 1913); director: Burton King

The Great Sacrifice (Kay-Bee, 1913)

Heart Throbs (ca. 1913)

The Heritage of Eve (Ince, 1913)

In the Days of the War (Pathe, 1913)

The Lost Dispatch (1913)

A Military Judas (1913)

Old Mammy's Secret Code (1913)

Pauline Cushman—The Federal Spy (Selig, 1913); director: Allan Dwan

The Picket Guard (1913); director: Allan Dwan

The Powder Flash of Death (Universal/Bison, 1913); director: Allan Dwan

The Pride of the South (Broncho, 1913)

The Sharpshooter (Ince, 1913)

Shenandoah (Kalem, 1913); director: Kenean Buel

Silent Heroes (Broncho, 1913)

The Sinews of War (1913)

A Slave's Devotion (1913)

Soldiers Three (Bison, 1913)

The Songbird of the North (Vitagraph, 1913)

Soul of the South (1913)

A Southern Cinderella (Ince, 1913)

The Toll of War (Bison, 1913)

The Volunteer Organist (Crescent, ca. 1913), 8 reels

The War Correspondent (ca. 1913)

When Lee Surrendered (ca. 1913)

When Lincoln Paid (ca. 1913)

When Lincoln Was President (Pilot, 1913)

With Lee in Virginia (ca. 1913)

Women and War (1913); director: Allan Dwan

The Baby Spy (Selig, 1914)

Between Two Fires (Lubin, 1914)

The Chest of Fortune (Kalem, 1914)

Dan (All-Star, 1914), 5 reels; directors: John H. Pratt and George Irving

The Fair Rebel (Biograph/Klaw & Erlanger, 1914); director: David Miles

Fitzhugh's Ride (Lubin, 1914); director: John E. Ince

In the Fall of '64 (Universal, 1914); director: Francis Ford

Lincoln the Lover (Vitagraph, 1914); director: Ralph Ince

The Littlest Rebel (Photoplay Prods., 1914), 6 reels; director: Edgar Lewis

Quantrell's Son (Vitagraph, 1914)

A Question of Courage (Majestic, 1914)

The Soul of Honor (Mutual, 1914)

The Southerners (Edison, 1914); directors: Richard Ridgely and John H. Collins

The Tavern of Tragedy (Majestic/Mutual, 1914); director: Donald Crisp

Uncle Tom's Cabin (World Producing Corp., 1914), 5 reels; director: William Robert Daly

Under Southern Skies (Universal, 1914)

Barbara Frietchie (Metro, 1915), 5 reels; director: Herbert Blache

The Birth of a Nation (Epoch Prod. Corp., 1915), 12 reels; director: D. W. Griffith

Colonel Carter of Cartersville (World Film Corp., 1915), 5 reels; director: Howell Hansell

The Coward (Triangle, 1915), 5 or 6 reels; director: Reginald Barker

A Gentle Volunteer (Rex, 1916)

The Heart of Lincoln (Universal, 1915), 3 reels; director: Francis Ford. Note: rereleased in 1922 by Anchor Film Distributors.

The Heart of Maryland (Tiffany, 1915), 6 reels; director: Herbert Brenon

The Life of Abraham Lincoln (Edison, 1915)

The Life of Sam Davis: A Confederate Hero of the Sixties (1915). Note: This film is unconfirmed; it may be the same film as *Sam Davis, the Hero of Tennessee,* listed below.

May Blossom (Paramount, 1915). 4 reels,
director: Allan Dwan

Rivals (Kalem, 1915)

Sam Davis, the Hero of Tennessee (Connor
Producing Co., 1915)

The Soul of the South (Kay-Bee, 1915)

Their One Love (Thanhouser, 1915)

Vain Justice (Essanay, 1915)

The Warrens of Virginia (Paramount,
1915), 5 reels; director: Cecil B.
DeMille

When Sherman Marched to the Sea (Bison,
1915)

The Crisis (Selig, 1916), 7 or 12 reels;
director: Colin Campbell

Her Father's Son (Paramount, 1916), 5
reels; director: William Desmond Taylor

Naked Hearts (1916)

Rose of the South (Vitagraph, 1916), 5
reels; director: Paul Scardon

Son of a Rebel Chief (Bison, 1916)

The Sting of Victory (Essanay, 1916), 5
reels; director: J. Charles Haydon

The Field of Honor (Universal, 1917), 5
reels; director: Allen J. Holubar

The Little Yank (Triangle, 1917), 5 reels;
director: George Siegmann

Seventy and Seven (1917)

The Spreading Dawn (Goldwyn, 1917), 5
reels; director: Lawrence Trimble

Those Without Sin (Paramount, 1917), 5
reels; director: Marshall Neilan

Your Obediant Servant (Edison, 1917)

Hearts of Love (General Film Corp., 1918),
6 reels; director: J. Charles Haydon

The Last Rebel (Triangle, 1918), 5 reels;
director: Gilbert R. Hamilton

Madam Who (W. W. Hodkinson/General
Film Corp., 1918), 7 reels; director:
Reginald Barker

Morgan's Raiders (Bluebird, 1918), 5 reels;
directors: Wilfred Lucas and Bess
Meredyth

Uncle Tom's Cabin (Paramount, 1918), 5
reels; director; J. Searle Dawley

Hay Foot, Straw Foot (Paramount, 1919),
5 reels; director: Jerome Storm

Salome Versus Shenandoah (Sennett,
1919)

Secret Service (Paramount, 1919), 6 reels;
director: Hugh Ford

The Copperhead (Paramount, 1920), 7
reels; director: Charles Maigne

Held by the Enemy (Paramount, 1920), 6
reels; director: Donald Crisp

The Kentucky Colonel (W. W.
Hodkinson/Pathe, 1920), 6 reels; director: William A. Seiter

The Little Shepherd of Kingdom Come
(Goldwyn, 1920), 6 reels; director:
Wallace Worsley

The Heart of Maryland (Vitagraph, 1921),
6 reels; director: Tom Terriss

The Highest Law (Selznick, 1921), 6 reels;
director: Ralph Ince

Jesse James Under the Black Flag (Mesco,
1921), 8 reels; director: Franklin B.
Coates

Johnny Ring and the Captain's Sword
(Temple Prods., 1921), 5 reels; director:
Norman L. Stevens